The Christological Controversy

Library of Congress Cataloging in Publication Data

Main entry under title:

The Christological controversy.

(Sources of early Christian thought)
Bibliography: p.
1. Jesus Christ—History of doctrines—Early church, ca. 30–600. I. Norris, Richard Alfred. II. Series.
BT198.C44   232'.09'015   79–8890
ISBN 0–8006–1411–9

Printed in the United States of America   1-1411

94   93   92   91   9   10

Contents

Series Foreword

Christianity has always been attentive to historical fact. Its motivation and focus have been, and continue to be, the span of life of one historical individual, Jesus of Nazareth, seen to be a unique historical act of God's self-communication. The New Testament declares that this Jesus placed himself within the context of the history of the people of Israel and perceived himself as the culmination of the revelation of the God of Israel, ushering into history a new chapter. The first followers of this Jesus and their succeeding generations saw themselves a part of this new history. Far more than a collection of teachings or a timeless philosophy, Christianity has been a movement in, and of, history, acknowledging its historical condition and not attempting to escape it.

Responsible scholarship now recognizes that Christianity has always been a more complex phenomenon than some have realized with a variety of worship services, theological languages, and structures of organization. Christianity assumed its variegated forms on the anvil of history. There is a real sense in which history is one of the shapers of Christianity. The view that development has occurred within Christianity during its history has virtually universal acceptance. But not all historical events had an equal influence on the development of Christianity. The historical experience of the first several centuries of Christianity shaped subsequent Christianity in an extremely crucial manner. It was in this initial phase that the critical features of the Christian faith were set; a vocabulary was created, options of belief and practice were accepted or rejected. Christianity's understanding of its God and of the person of Christ, its worship life, its communal structure, its understand-

vii

ing of the human condition, all were largely resolved in this early period, known as the time of the church fathers or the patristic church (A.D. 100–700). Because this is the case, both those individuals who bring a faith commitment to Christianity and those interested in it as a major religious and historical phenomenon must have a special regard for what happened to the Christian faith in these pivotal centuries.

The purpose of this series is to allow an English-reading public to gain firsthand insights into these significant times for Christianity by making available in a modern, readable English the fundamental sources which chronicle how Christianity and its theology attained their normative character. Whenever possible, entire patristic writings or sections are presented. The varying points of view within the early church are given their opportunity to be heard. An introduction by the translator and editor of each volume describes the context of the documents for the reader.

Hopefully these several volumes will enable their readers to gain not only a better understanding of the early church but also an appreciation of how Christianity of the twentieth century still reflects the events, thoughts, and social conditions of this earlier history.

It has been pointed out repeatedly that the problem of doctrinal development within the church is basic to ecumenical discussion today. If this view is accepted, along with its corollary that historical study is needed, then an indispensable element of true ecumenical responsibility has to be a more extensive knowledge of patristic literature and thought. It is with that urgent concern, as well as a regard for a knowledge of the history of Christianity, that *Sources of Early Christian Thought* is published.

WILLIAM G. RUSCH

The Christological Controversy

I.

Introduction

This book is a collection of texts designed to illustrate the development of Christian thought about the person of Christ in the era of the church fathers. The earliest text translated comes from the latter half of the second century, when the ideas and problems which were to dominate christological thought in this period were first crystallized. The latest is the well-known "Definition of the Faith" of the Council of Chalcedon (A.D. 451), which has generally been accepted as defining the limits of christological orthodoxy.

EARLY CHRISTOLOGY

Christianity appeared on the stage of history as a movement with a message of salvation. Its preachers announced that God was bringing "the restoration of all things" (Acts 3:21)—the new age promised by the prophets—when wrong would be righted and humanity reconciled to God. This proclamation was rooted in the life and ministry of Jesus of Nazareth, who himself had come preaching the near advent of the kingdom of God, God's definitive assertion of his rule. He had apparently seen his own ministry as a sign, a significant anticipation, of that coming redemption.

Early Christian preaching, however, was not based simply on the message of Jesus. Rather, it grew out of the conviction that the content of his message had been both validated and actualized through his resurrection from the dead. The powers which rule the present world order had repudiated Jesus and slain him. But God had raised him up, and this meant that in him and for him the promised transformation of the world, "the life of the age to come," was already real. Furthermore, it meant that people could even now have a foretaste of that new life because the Spirit of God had, through Jesus, been bestowed on those who accepted him as the one in whom their own destiny was revealed and determined.

Thus there were from the very beginning two things to be said about Jesus. The first was that God's salvation, the thing to which prophets and seers had always looked forward, had, for Jesus, already become real. He already belonged to that new order of things. The second was that Jesus was the one through whom others entered into the new order of things; he was the bearer of God's rule, the mediator of God's salvation. In short he was, in the Christian sense of that term, the Messiah, the Christ, the Son of God.

Here we can see what is meant by "Christology." That term does not signify just any sort of inquiry or reflection which has Jesus as its object. It refers quite specifically to inquiry and reflection that are concerned with Jesus *in his messianic character*. In other words, Christology asks what is presupposed and implied by the fact that Jesus is the elect "Son of God," the one through whose life, death, and resurrection God has acted to realize his purpose for humanity; and this fact imposes, from the beginning, a certain logic on Christology. To understand or evaluate Jesus christologically means, on the one hand, to ask about his relation to God and, on the other, to seek a way of expressing his representative character as a human being—his status as the one in whom humanity's common destiny is both summed up and determined.

The earliest Christian literature reveals differing ways of accounting for Jesus in his messianic character. It may well be the case that the earliest Christology simply proclaimed Jesus as the human being who had been marked out by the resurrection as the coming Messiah, that is, as the one through whom God would finally set things right. In such a Christology, the title "Son of God" would have referred not to any quality of divinity but to the fact that Jesus was called and set apart for a certain function in God's purposes. In fact, however, this way of understanding Jesus was generally supplanted as Christianity spread among Greek-speaking peoples in the Mediterranean world.

The movement of thought which occurred can perhaps best be

studied in Paul's letters, the earliest Christian writings available to us. There we can observe at least three important developments in the portrayal of Jesus. In the first place, he is proclaimed not just as the Messiah who is to come but also as the present "Lord" both of the Christian community and of the cosmos. His resurrection marks him as the one in whom, even now, the powers of the new creation are operative. He is thus a heavenly figure, the embodiment of God's eternal purposes for humanity and the universal agent of those purposes. In the second place, and naturally enough, all that Jesus was and did from the very beginning of his earthly ministry is understood as the expression of God's will and the product of God's initiative. Paul insists that the very presence of Jesus among us was the result of a divine act of "sending" (Gal. 4:4) and that he came "to redeem those who were under the law" (Gal. 4:5). The ministry of Jesus is then itself God's working out of his purposes for humanity: "In Christ God was reconciling the world to himself" (2 Cor. 5:19). Finally, the early church began to think of Jesus in his earthly ministry as the human presence "with us" (Matt. 1:23) of the Son of God—the heavenly being who is the expression of God's very self and therefore of his will for his creatures. What Jesus was revealed to be by his resurrection is what Jesus always had been: "life-giving spirit" (1 Cor. 15:45).

The product of these lines of thought can be discerned in two early Christian hymns quoted in the Pauline corpus. In Philippians, Paul reminds his readers that the Christ, "though he was in the form of God, did not count equality with God a thing to be grasped, but emptied himself, taking the form of a servant, being born in the likeness of men" (Phil. 2:6-7). He is citing what was doubtless a well-known form of words, and he refers to it in order to commend humility and charity to his readers. In the process, he gives us a glimpse of the christological beliefs which were current in his churches. The Christ is a heavenly figure who was "in the form of God" and who enters the world as a human being in order to bring salvation. In the letter to the Colossians, the identity of this heavenly figure is clarified. "He is the image of the invisible God, the firstborn of all creation; for in him all things were created, in heaven and on earth. . . . He is before all things, and in him all things hold together" (Col. 1:15–17). The Christ, in fact, is the personified divine Wisdom, the living expression of all that God is and all that God wills, and the one through whom God carries out his works. It is this Wisdom who is with people in Jesus. Jesus thus appears as the human being in whom the divine power which sustains the cosmos and embodies God's design for humanity becomes actively present for the sake of redemption.

This is the Christology which quickly came to dominate Christian thought about Jesus. It surfaces in its definitive New Testament form in John's Gospel, where Jesus is understood as the creative Logos or "Word" of God who "became flesh" to make "grace and truth" manifest (see John 1:1–14). It appears also in Hebrews, where the Son of God is described as the one through whom God "created the world" and who "reflects the glory of God and bears the very stamp of his nature" (Heb. 1:2–3). In the last resort, the New Testament cannot make sense of Jesus except by seeing his human life as the historical concretion of the very power through which God originally expressed himself in the creation of the world. Only in this way, it seemed, could one account for the truly universal significance of his life, death, and resurrection, or the truly ultimate and definitive character of the salvation which he brought.

What is true of the writings of the New Testament is true also of other early Christian literature. For example, the First Epistle of Clement, a product of the Roman church at the end of the first century, tells us that "according to the flesh" the Lord Jesus Christ is the descendant of Jacob (1 Clement 32.2); but he is also the Son of the Father God and the "radiance of his majesty," so that he can confer on people knowledge of the ultimate light (1 Clement 36; cf. 59.1). Another document from the Roman church, the so-called *Shepherd of Hermas*, says "The Holy Spirit which exists beforehand, which created the whole creation, God settled in the flesh which he willed" (*Hermas, Similitudes* 5.6.5). In Hermas's mind, this Holy Spirit is the same as the Son of God, whom the author also "sees" in his vision as a "glorious man" (*ibid.*, 9.7.1; cf. 9.6.1) and indeed as the greatest of the seven angels (*ibid.*, 9.12.6–8). Through him the others have access to the presence of God. He is "older than all his creation, so that he was the counselor of his creation to the Father" (*ibid.*, 9.12.2). For Hermas, then, Christ is Spirit, Son, Man, and Angel—a somewhat confusing set of descriptions. Nevertheless, his basic meaning is clear. Jesus somehow comes into our world from God's world as "Spirit" and "Angel." But he is not just any member of the divine order. He is the Spirit and Angel *par excellence*—the one who was God's counselor and helper in creation, like God's Wisdom and Word in the Old Testament.

The same essential pattern of christological thought can be found in the writings of Ignatius of Antioch, who in A.D.113 wrote seven letters to a series of local churches as he traveled under guard to his martyrdom at Rome. For Ignatius, Jesus Christ is God's "Word proceeding from silence" (*Magnesians* 8.2). At the same time, he is of David's lineage and the son of Mary; he was born and ate and drank and suffered and was "truly raised from the dead" (*Trallians* 9.1–2). These assertions, which are made in part for polemical reasons, can all be summed up for Ignatius in the statement that Jesus Christ "was in the presence of the Father before the ages and appeared at the end" (*Magn.* 7.1) or in the assertion, "There is one physician, fleshly and spiritual, generate and ungenerate, God in a human being, true life in death, both from Mary and from God, first subject to suffering and then incapable of suffering, Jesus Christ our Lord" (*Ephesians* 7.2).

The thought of Clement, Ignatius, and Hermas moves along the same basic lines as that of the New Testament writers. It accounts for Jesus and the salvation which he brings by speaking of the incarnation of one who is God's proper self-expression, God's Son. There results a portrayal of Jesus as having a dual character—as embodying in himself the unity of two ways of being, spiritual and fleshly, divine and human. This picture establishes the starting point, provides the essential paradigm, and, above all, dictates an agenda for later patristic Christology.

INITIAL PROBLEMS

To say that this early picture of Jesus dictated an agenda for later Christology is merely to say that, when examined closely and expounded seriously, it raised a whole series of knotty questions.

They in turn gave rise to critical and systematic thought about the person of Christ. The beginnings of this process are to be sought in the second century, when two distinct sets of christological issues were raised and debated. The first of these concerned the nature and identity of the heavenly "power" which was said to have become incarnate as, or in, Jesus. The second was created by denials of the reality of Jesus' "flesh," that is, his ordinary human nature.

Justin Martyr

Issues concerning the incarnate heavenly power were focused by the emergence of the so-called Logos-theology appearing in the writings of the second-century Apologists. It plays a central role in the thought of Justin Martyr, who taught in Rome around the middle of the second century. Justin in effect takes up the language of John 1:1–14, where, as we have seen, Jesus is described as the enfleshed Logos or "Word" of God. This Logos is God's Son, a reality distinct from the Father but begotten of him for the creation of the world. As Justin understands it, it was the Logos who made God known to the people of the old covenant, even as it was he who, in the last days, became a human being—body, soul, and spirit (1 *Apology* 10.1). The Logos came down in lowliness and humiliation, as the prophets had taught, but he will have a second coming, in glory, when he will judge the world and establish the Father's kingdom.

There is nothing very new in any of this—as Justin himself, who learned it from his own Christian teachers, would have insisted. What is new is the understanding of the Logos which Justin develops in his role as a Christian philosopher—an understanding for which he draws on contemporary Platonist and Stoic thought.

For Justin, "logos" meant essentially "reason." The term referred, in accordance with traditional Stoic teaching, to the indwelling, active, formative principle of the cosmos—the divine power which orders and maintains the world-system. This divine reason, however, was not the first or ultimate deity. It was derivative, "begotten." Logos was the divine reason uttered as the divine Word for the sake of forming and governing the world. As such, of

6

course, it was perfectly expressive of God's being and purposes. It was like a fire lit from the fire that is God. Nevertheless, it was derivative, and for that reason inferior to the one God.

In Justin's thought the Logos was the mediator between God and his creatures. The indescribable, incomprehensible Creator touches the world only through his derivative self-expression. It is the Logos who forms the universe, who "appears" to Abraham and Moses, and who confers knowledge of God on all humanity by giving people a share in God's rational nature. It becomes understandable, therefore, that it is the Logos who, in the person of Jesus, becomes incarnate to overcome the forces of demonic unreason and to open the way to a new life for humanity.

This careful development of the Logos-doctrine immediately created problems. Those who opposed it openly—the "Monarchians," as they were called, because of their devotion to the idea that God is one—saw it as a clear threat to monotheism. It seemed to introduce plurality into the divine realm. In fact, of course, this was not quite true. In Justin's system there truly was, in the last resort, only one ultimate God. The Logos represented a slightly lower level of divinity, something between the pure divinity of God and the nondivinity of creatures. Justin had made sense of the incarnational picture of Jesus by adopting a hierarchical picture of the world-order in which the Logos stands as a kind of bumper state between God and the world, and it is this fact that makes Justin's Christology problematic. For one thing, it raises the question, What exactly do Christians mean by the term *mediator* as that is applied to Jesus? Is the mediator simply the Logos himself, a natural halfway house between God and humanity? Or is the mediator one in whom God and humanity are somehow directly together with each other? If the latter is the case, then Justin's Logos-doctrine represents a serious misunderstanding. Also, his teaching inevitably raises the question of why God should need a middleman to stand between himself and the created order. Does Justin think that God cannot enter into direct relationship with "flesh"? That is what his hierarchical picture of the world seems to imply.

For Justin this thought is truly no more than an unexplored

7

possibility. Other second-century thinkers, however, openly argued that it is inconceivable for a being who properly belongs to the realm of the divine to take ordinary human flesh. These thinkers, called "Docetists" because they described Jesus' flesh as mere "appearance," believed that there is an absolute contrariety between God and the material order, which they pictured as the independent creation of a second and evil, or inferior, God. One consequence of this radical dualism was a particular understanding of the meaning of redemption. Certain Gnostic thinkers who claimed to teach the true meaning of the apostles' message insisted that redemption meant the extrication of the "spiritual" part of men and women from the material world in which it had been trapped. Naturally enough, given this view of salvation, they were unwilling to acknowledge that the divine Savior had taken authentic flesh. Instead they tended to suggest that the human Jesus was simply shadowed or accompanied by the true Christ—who, therefore, was exempt from such indignities as birth, hunger, suffering, and death. Others, like Marcion of Pontus, argued that the flesh of Jesus was phantasmal. None of these thinkers wanted to deny the presence for human beings of the revealer of the ultimate God, but they did want to deny that he could ever have been an actual part of the spatial and temporal order.

Behind this view there lay a repudiation of the Old Testament God—the God who, according to Genesis, was responsible for the present, intolerable order of things. This rejection of the Jewish God, however, was merely an expression of a deep sense of alienation from the world which is the present context of human existence. For Marcion and people who saw things as he did, there was something so evil in things as they are that the true God could not be associated with them in any way—and for just this reason, God's Logos could not be thought to suffer incarnation.

In two different ways, then, the second century brought to the surface serious issues about the traditional interpretation of Jesus and his work. On the one hand, Justin's Logos-theology made it necessary to ask whether the incarnational Christology really intended to assert that Jesus is "God with us"—or, to put it another way, whether a mediatorial Logos, when he becomes incarnate, can honestly be understood as God present in person. On the other hand, Marcion and the Gnostic movement raised the question of whether the whole idea of incarnation might not be a contradiction in terms, that perhaps "flesh" is precisely the evil with which God can have nothing to do.

Melito of Sardis

It is in the context of these problems that the christological ideas of Melito of Sardis must be examined, representing as they do a persuasive presentation of the traditional position.

Melito himself is an obscure figure. Until very recently he was known only through the references to him in Eusebius's *Ecclesiastical History* and through certain fragments of his writings quoted by later authors. In 1940, however, there appeared a printed edition of a nearly complete manuscript of Melito's newly discovered *Homily on the Passover,* and since that time further manuscripts have appeared which enable a full reproduction of its text.

This work, as even a quick reading will reveal, is of interest in a number of different ways. It is one of the earliest Christian sermons we possess. It is also important for an understanding of early Christian exegesis of Scripture and of the relations between early Christianity and Judaism. For our purposes, however, its interest lies in its portrayal of Christ. Here we have at first glance an eloquent statement of the christological tradition which depends ultimately on the thought of Paul and the author of the Fourth Gospel. For Melito, Christ is a glorious, divine figure who becomes incarnate for the sake of the redemption of humankind from the suffering and death which were its inheritance from Adam. Moreover, this incarnation or embodiment of the Son of God is the fulfillment of the whole dispensation of the Mosaic convenant, which is, for Melito, not only a salvific work of God in its own right but a "type" or foreshadowing of the perfect salvation given in Christ.

In working out this typological exegesis of the Exodus narrative and thus weaving the history of Christ and that of Israel into a single whole, Melito is consciously or unconsciously taking a stand against Docetism. Not only did Marcion and certain Gnostic teachers repudiate the Jewish Scriptures, but they also denied that the true God had been active or revealed in any moment of the history of Moses and the prophets. Melito, on the other hand, is obliged by his very exegetical method to attach significance to the history of the people of God prior to the advent of Christ. He discerns a fundamental unity in history, rooted in the fact that "God's firstborn" called and guided Israel, and indeed humanity, from the time of creation to that of the incarnation.

Melito's awareness of the problems represented by Marcion's teaching and that of the Gnostics is also revealed in his insistence on the reality of the physical dimension of the incarnation. Melito insists that God's Son "put on" or "dressed in" a human being and genuinely "suffered for the sake of" sufferers (*Hom.* 100). It is he who was tied up and who died and who was entombed. Melito asks no questions about how this can be so. He merely asserts that "he who made the heaven and the earth," that is, the divine Word who is also called God's Son, "was enfleshed in the virgin" (*Hom.* 104), and he uses language calculated to emphasize the seriousness with which both sorts of statements about Jesus are made—those which identify him as "Alpha and Omega," and those which present him as an ordinary human being.

Irenaeus of Lyon

These same themes are touched upon in much more explicit form in the writings of Irenaeus of Lyon. Born in Asia Minor probably around A.D. 140, Irenaeus at some point in his life moved to the southern part of Gaul. There he became prominent in the Christian community, and as a presbyter of the church at Lyon carried a message from the martyrs there to Eleutherius, the bishop of Rome. On his return from this embassy, Irenaeus was elected bishop of Lyon, taking the place of one Pothinus, who had been martyred in the great upsurge of local hostility to Christians. While bishop, he wrote the work for which he has been remembered ever since: the work he entitled *A Detection and Refutation of the Falsely Named "Knowledge"* but which history has rather called simply *Against Heresies*. This long, meandering composition in five books is in fact a direct attack on Marcion and on other teachers and groups which Irenaeus lumps together as "Gnostic." Concerning the date of this work, we can say only that it appeared after A.D. 180. It was extremely influential in its own time, as is evidenced by the fact that it was almost immediately translated into Latin from its original language, Greek. It is the Latin text which is known today, since the Greek is available only in fragments.

Irenaeus sees the basic difficulty in Marcionite and Gnostic thought to lie in the denial of true divinity to the Creator of the world. The allegation that there are "two Gods"—or at any rate that the true God, the ultimate Father, has no responsibility for or involvement in the material, temporal world—is for Irenaeus the typical, and in that sense definitive, teaching of Marcion and the Gnostics. He recognizes, however, that the dualism which surfaces in this idea shows up in other forms as well: in a denial of continuity between the history of Israel and the Christian dispensation, for example, and in Christology, where it results in a belief in two Christs, a heavenly Christ and an earthly Christ, the former of whom only seems to have a physical or material embodiment.

Confronted by this dualism, Irenaeus replies with what is essentially an assertion not only of the identity of the ultimate God with the Creator but also of the intimate involvement of God himself with the creaturely, and therefore the material, order. This pair of emphases is seen in his Christology in three ways.

In the first place, it is seen in his way of understanding who and what the Word or Son of God is. Irenaeus is a conscious heir of the teachings of Justin Martyr. He is not, however, at ease with the idea of a mediatorial Logos—not only because such a conception seems to introduce plurality into the divine realm but also because it seems to set God apart from the world. Irenaeus likes to emphasize that God "takes a hand" directly in the world, and when he talks about the Logos, he often describes him as a "hand" of God, as a way in which God is present in the world. In Irenaeus's Christology, therefore, emphasis is laid on what we might call the fullness of Christ's divinity, and mediation is accomplished not so much because the divine Son has an "in between" way of being as because the divine Son takes on the human way of being. It is the incarnation itself which is the mediation.

The incarnation, however, is not for Irenaeus the only instance of God's being present for people in his Word or Logos. On the contrary, the Scriptures of the old covenant reveal that all human history, from the time of the creation of Adam and Eve, is the story of the working out of God's purpose for humanity through a series of "dispensations." By these God brings the human race to knowledge of himself—a knowledge which, as it is attained, transforms people and lifts them up to a new kind of life. Through Word and Spirit, God brings the creatures he shaped out of earth to share in his own way of being and thus to live *with* him, in his presence. For Irenaeus, therefore, the incarnation "sums up," or "recapitulates" what God has always been doing for people. By the same token, the incarnation, or rather Christ himself, sums up and recapitulates all that humanity is and will be for God. The incarnation is the point at which the beginning and the end of human existence are focused in one human life, the human life of God's Logos.

Thus, finally, incarnation is real for Irenaeus just because it represents the unity of God with humanity and the unity of human history with God. God the Logos takes to himself in Christ the being of Adam—the being of flesh, of materiality. This is the theme that is most prominent in the christological passages which have been translated here from *Against Heresies*. The "dual" Christ which Irenaeus finds in Gnostic teaching is repudiated in favor of a Christ who is the unity of the divine and the creaturely. This mediator breaks the power of Satan—the power which keeps humanity subject to sin and to dissolution—by reversing Adam's original disobedience. In this way the mediator sets the stage for the transformation of humanity by the work of the Holy Spirit— the process of redemption.

Tertullian of Carthage

The issues Irenaeus faced and dealt with in *Against Heresies* were still real in the next generation. This is apparent from the passages excerpted here from the two treatises of Tertullian, *Against Praxeas* and *On the Flesh of Christ*. Tertullian himself came from an entirely different sector of the Mediterranean world than Irenaeus. He was a Latin-speaking North African, with the education of a rhetorician and a lawyer. Carthage was the place of his birth and of his mature career as a Christian writer, which began around 195 and ceased with his death around 220. His primary concern was with the calling of the church to be pure in its obedience to God's law and God's teachings in the midst of a hostile and dying world. This concern led him to write continually on moral and doctrinal problems. Indeed, it led him eventually out of the Catholic church altogether and into the fellowship of the Montanist movement, whose ideals and standards for Christian life were closer to his own.

The two issues that prompted Tertullian to write on matters of Christology were precisely those of which we spoke in the last section: those created by the Logos-theology of Justin and those created by the dualism of Marcion and the Gnostics.

It is the latter whom Tertullian has in mind in his treatise *On the Flesh of Christ,* which had a companion piece in another essay, *On the Resurrection of the Flesh.* His protagonists were those who denied that redemption or salvation involves the whole human person, body as well as soul or spirit, and who consequently saw no need for the divine Son to be involved with real flesh. The basic issue for Tertullian, therefore, was the question whether the salvation which the term "resurrection" symbolizes included the physical as well as the nonphysical parts of human nature. In dealing with this problem, he does not simply attack his opponents for making the incarnation, in effect, a masquerade. He realizes that the ultimate issue is that of the value, and therefore the redeemability, of the physical order. Consequently, his strongest argument is one in which, against Marcion, he insists upon the fact that flesh, even with all its weakness and ugliness, is an object of God's love; and for Tertullian this fact counts for more than Marcion's— not to mention his own—distaste for the body.

This repudiation of dualism goes hand in hand, for Tertullian, with a defense of the Logos-doctrine as he had received it from Greek-speaking Christian authors. His defense, undertaken at some length in the treatise *Against Praxeas,* was directed by Tertullian the Montanist against people who wanted to assert the absolute unity of the divine in face of the apparent division and plurality which the Logos-doctrine introduced into the divine nature. These "Monarchians" accepted a doctrine of incarnation, but since they held to the unitary nature of God, they had to insist that it was God himself who was incarnate in Christ—an idea which shocked Tertullian, who accused his foes of making the Creator himself subject to suffering and death. His own position was that deity is absolutely one in its nature (in the "spirit" which constitutes it) but threefold in the way that its being is, so to speak, organized or articulated. Tertullian employs images like that of a fountain and the stream which issues from it, or a light and its radiance, to explain the difference between Father and Son in the Godhead. He believes that the Son or Word was projected by God for the purpose of creating and ordering the world, that this same Son or Word was the revealer of God in the dispensation of the old covenant, and that he finally became incarnate as Jesus of Nazareth for the salvation of humankind.

What is important about the treatise *Against Praxeas* is that in it Tertullian not only develops a christological vocabulary which was to influence later thought but also appears as the first Christian thinker to raise the question of how the person of the incarnate Logos should be described. In chapter 27 of the treatise, he turns his attention to the Monarchian account of the distinction between Father and Son. His opponents had maintained that "Son" refers to the humanity of Jesus, his flesh, while "Father" refers to his deity. This troubled Tertullian because, while he insisted upon distinguishing Logos and Father within the sphere of the divine, he did not believe that Jesus Christ, the incarnate Logos, is two separate things or items—*personae*. There is only one of him, Tertullian argues, and he expresses this judgment by saying that Christ is one "person." Of course, he sees a duality in Christ. Jesus is constituted out of two "substances," flesh on the one hand and Spirit on the other, which are designations for human and divine ways of being. In him, these factors are mingled, though not in such a way as to react on one another and be mutually changed. The two substances continue unaltered in the one person and provide the bases for two kinds of activity, human and divine.

Origen of Alexandria

With Origen, Tertullian's younger contemporary, we step back into the world of Greek Christianity. The successor of Pantaenus

14

and Clement of Alexandria as head of the catechetical school at Alexandria in Egypt, Origen ended his days in Palestinian Caesarea after a difference with his bishop had forced him from his home. Origen's life was devoted to study and to exposition of the meaning of the Christian and Jewish Scriptures. In them he found a wisdom which not only enabled people to enter into the mysteries of God's being and action but also showed them the way to their self-fulfillment in the knowledge of God through his Wisdom or Logos. At the same time, Origen was learned in the traditions of Greek philosophy. In the history of philosophy, he belongs on the borderline between Middle Platonism and Neoplatonism. His learning and critical ability made him a sensitive and constructive apologist for Christianity—though always within the framework of the sort of eclectic Platonism which he had inherited from his teacher Clement and from Philo, the great Jewish philosopher of Alexandria.

In the book titled *On First Principles*, a work of his youth, Origen sets out from the teaching tradition of the church, first expounding its basic contents and then dealing with the problems it raised for him and his contemporaries. In this process he lays the foundation both for an understanding of the Logos-doctrine and for an account of the person and function of Jesus.

Origen believed, as against his predecessors, that God begets his Wisdom or Logos eternally—that there never was a time when the Logos did not exist (*De prin.* 1.2.9). This divine Wisdom, moreover, is the complete expression of God's being. At the same time, Wisdom is not God himself but his image, a "second God," subordinate to the ultimate Father of all.

In this character, the Logos is the mediator between God and the created order, and first of all in the act of creation itself. Through his agency, God brings into being an immaterial cosmos of rational spirits, intelligences whose whole being is focused on the loving contemplation of God through his Wisdom. However, since these intelligences are finite and changeable and possessed of freedom, they can and do fall away from God—away from unity into dispersion, away from eternity into time, away from the immaterial into the material. God accordingly creates for them an ordered

15

physical universe, a kind of second-best cosmos. This visible world, set in harmonious order by God's Wisdom, then becomes the scene of their redemption—their slow education back to that knowledge of God in which alone their being is fulfilled. In order that this may occur, however, Wisdom the mediator must be mediated to the fallen spirits, and this is the point of the incarnation.

The first stage in this process of mediation is fulfilled through the unification of the Logos with the one rational spirit which did not fall away from God—the soul which is Jesus. The mode of this union, as Origen sees it, is contemplative love. The unfallen soul's love for Wisdom is so intense that it identifies itself in and with God's eternal image of himself, and so becomes the expression, the mediator, of Wisdom. To explain what sort of union this is, Origen resorts to a classical philosophical illustration of the mixture or blending of two substances, the case of iron set in a fire. As the iron acquires all the qualities of fire, and indeed is interpenetrated and transformed by the fire without ceasing to be iron, so the soul which is Jesus is assimilated to the divine Wisdom, the Logos, and thus reveals and conveys Wisdom.

The second stage in the mediation comes when this soul which is united to the Logos becomes embodied through a human birth. Even the body, in Origen's eyes, is elevated in virtue of its unity with God's Wisdom. For example, it can be transfigured, as the Gospels tell us, and become transparent to the glory of God. Yet it is and remains body. As such it becomes the means by which the Logos signifies himself to sense-bound intelligences, as well as the means by which they begin their intellectual ascent beyond body to the Logos in his own being.

In this scheme there are many points of interest. One matter stands out from the point of view of future developments. Origen shares Justin's sense of the need for mediation between God and the visible and spiritual creation. His universe too is hierarchical, and consequently the divine does not mix too directly with matter. As the Logos mediates God to the soul, so the soul mediates God's Son to the body. It is the necessity for this double mediation which, at least apparently, explains the unique form of Origen's picture of Christ's person. Jesus is a human being (soul inhabiting body), perfectly united as intelligence with its original, the divine Intelligence or Wisdom.

FURTHER PROBLEMS

Origen's understanding of Christ fits closely together with his Platonist world-picture and with his consequent view of the status and character of the Logos. The next stage in the development of patristic Christology was occasioned by the Arian controversy, in which just this question—that of the status and character of the Logos—was at stake. The issue, as we have seen, was implicitly raised by Justin's formulation of the Logos-doctrine, and it occasioned some discomfort to Irenaeus. It came to a head with the teaching of Arius and his followers.

The Arians and Athanasius

Everyone understood that the Logos or Wisdom of God was divine. It was not clear, however, exactly what that term "divine" meant. For example, it might denote a quality of which there can be degrees, and on such an understanding it would be consistent to say that the Logos is divine and yet not God in the same sense, to the same degree, as the Father. This understanding seems to be implicit in the teaching of Justin and is explicit in that of Origen. We have seen, however, that the hierarchical vision of things which such a view involves implies a God who cannot and does not "mix" with the created order. It also calls into question the doctrine laid down by Justin himself, that the characteristics of deity belong only to one—namely, God himself.

Arius, the Alexandrian presbyter whose public teaching after A.D. 318 occasioned the trinitarian and christological debates of the fourth century, was a firm believer not only in the unity of God but also in a doctrine of divine transcendence which saw God's way of being as inconsistent with that of the created order. Logically enough, therefore, his doctrine of the Logos was so formulated as to express two convictions: first, that the Logos cannot be God in the proper sense; second, that the Logos performs an essential mediatorial role in the relation of God to world. He taught, accor-

17

dingly, that the Logos belongs to the created order but at the same time that he is a quite superior creature, ranking above all others because he was brought into being by God "before the ages" to act as the agent of God in creation. It was this doctrine which the Council of Nicaea (A.D. 325) repudiated in its famous creed, which declared that the Logos is not a creature but is eternally born out of God himself and is therefore divine in the same sense as the Father (*homoousios tōi theōi*).

These statements, of course, do not present themselves as strictly christological in bearing. They touch, at least formally, not on the incarnation but on the being and nature of God. Nevertheless, they have implications for Christology, and the reason this is so can be seen if we look at a writing on the incarnation which was composed without reference to the Arian controversy.

In his famous treatise *On the Incarnation of the Logos of God*, the bishop of Alexandria, Athanasius, tried to answer the question "Why?" with regard to the incarnation. His answer was basically that the Logos made a human body his own in order to restore humanity to the state which God had originally intended for the human race. Human beings, constituted of soul together with body, had been created to share the qualities of God's own life by living in fellowship with their Creator—by knowing him, and through such knowledge being conformed, at their own creaturely level, to his way of being. In sin they had turned away from the knowledge of God, and in consequence two things happened. In their bodies they became subject to physical death, and in their souls they were subjected to that spiritual death which consists in the loss of their character as reflections—images—of God's being.

Restoration, then, means overcoming people's liability to death and restoring their character as true reflections and images of God. This the Logos accomplishes in two ways. First, by his death on the cross he discharges the debt which had rendered human beings morally liable to physical death. Second, by his presence he enables people to share in the divine life. That sharing, as Athanasius understood it, has two dimensions. It means, of course, immortality and incorruptibility for people in their bodily nature, but above all it means the rediscovery of their true selves, their true spiritual identity, in the Logos himself, the proper and perfect image of God.

This account of the rationale of the incarnation has immediate implications for an understanding of Christ's person. Human beings, it holds, find themselves in God. Their true selfhood lies in their assimilation to God and their sharing in his way of being. For Athanasius, therefore, redemption can occur only through God's active presence with people. The incarnation is and must be the incarnation of one who is fully and truly God. Inevitably, then, Athanasius repudiated the teaching of Arius on christological, and not merely theological, grounds. His understanding of redemption made no sense if the Logos was a being "between" the divine and the human. It made sense only if the Logos was God's way of being personally present and active in the world.

In this teaching there is an implicit criticism of the whole of the early Logos-theology. Athanasius stands with Irenaeus in thinking that there must be a real and direct union of God with humanity in Christ. In insisting on this point, however, Athanasius created another problem for himself, for the Arians could argue, as apparently they did, that the things said about Jesus in the Gospels are not things one can say about the Logos if the Logos is truly God. For example, Jesus is said to have been hungry, to have felt emotions like sorrow and anger, to have asked questions which presupposed ignorance, and to have died. Are these characteristics really consistent with the hypothesis that the Logos is God? Do they not rather tend to show that he is a creature?

These questions embody two important assumptions. The first is that in the person of Jesus the Logos is the sole real subject. Whatever Jesus says or does or suffers comes from or affects the Logos, for the Logos *is* the "self" in Jesus. Thus the Arian questions presuppose a view of the person of Christ which is quite unlike Origen's. They assume that Logos incarnate is to be understood on the analogy of soul embodied: that Jesus is simply divine Logos together with a body and hence that no human soul is involved in his constitution. The second assumption is that of a basic inconsistency between God's way of being and that of human persons.

They are not merely different but also logically irreconcilable. It is unthinkable that God should be affected by physical conditions of any sort or that he should share in human emotion or human ignorance. This is consonant with what we have already seen of Arian theology. In this case, however, the assumption governs a strictly christological position.

In the third of his *Orations against the Arians*, portions of which are translated here, Athanasius, now speaking both as the bishop of Alexandria and as leader of the anti-Arian forces in the church, addresses himself to these Arian questions about the implications of the doctrine that "the Logos became flesh." As far as we can tell, this long and careful work was written during Athanasius's third exile, which he spent with the monks of the Egyptian desert. This means that it was written between A.D. 358 and 362. The patriarch tries to answer the Arian christological challenge by making a distinction between the Logos *in himself* and the Logos *with his flesh* or body. Tears, hunger, ignorance, and the like do not belong to the Logos in himself; they belong to him by virtue of his incarnate state. They are proper to the flesh which is proper to the Logos. One might say, therefore, that they belong to him only indirectly (though not, for that reason, the less truly).

It is clear from this brief account of Athanasius's basic argument that he shares with the Arians not their view of the Logos, but their view of the constitution of Jesus' person. He argues explicitly that it is wrong to perceive the incarnation as the Logos' indwelling of a whole human being. That, he thinks, would make the incarnation a case of mere inspiration. No, in the incarnation what happened was that the Logos took to himself—made his own—"flesh" or "body" or what we might call "the human condition" and so became the self or subject in Jesus. Naturally enough, therefore, Athanasius does not mention a human soul—a conscious human selfhood—in Jesus. For practical purposes, he regards Jesus, as the Arians did, as Logos plus body or flesh (though he nowhere openly denies that Jesus had a human soul).

The result of this is that when Athanasius has to deal with the question of Jesus' ignorance, his account of the matter inevitably seems strained. Unlike physical suffering, for example, or hunger, ignorance was not ordinarily attributed to the physical frame of a human being. Consequently, Athanasius had to account for Jesus' ignorance by suggesting that for purposes of the incarnation the Logos restrained himself and did not exhibit his omniscience; he acted "as if" he were a human being. This in turn, however, seems—at least to the modern reader—to call into question the full reality of Jesus' humanity. Athanasius was certainly not in the ordinary sense a Docetist. He did not question the reality of the flesh which the Logos took. Even so, his position suggests that Jesus was less than a complete human being.

Apollinaris of Laodicea

In speaking of the argument of Athanasius, we must emphasize that Athanasius merely *suggests* this idea. He does not raise, and so does not explicitly answer, the question whether Jesus did or did not have a human center of consciousness. The man who raised that question—and answered it in the negative in accordance with the "Logos-flesh" model for the person of Jesus—was Apollinaris of Laodicea, a friend of Athanasius and a firm enemy of Arianism, who in the course of a long career in the fourth century earned a significant reputation both as a devout ascetic and as a learned interpreter of the Scriptures. Teaching in Antioch, Apollinaris wrote in opposition to the Christology of teachers there who thought of the incarnation as a special case of the Logos' indwelling of a human being. Replying to this Christology, Apollinaris evolved an understanding of Christ which emphasized the unity of his person as "one incarnate nature of the divine Logos."

Because he was eventually condemned as a heretic, Apollinaris's writings were not circulated openly. Many of them are known only because they are quoted by his opponents, whether contemporary writers like Gregory of Nyssa or later authors like Theodoret of Cyrrhus and Leontius of Byzantium. It is from these authors that we have the group of fragments translated here. Some of his works, however, were preserved by his followers, who transmitted them under pseudonyms. Thus the treatise *On the Union in Christ of the Body with the Godhead* once circulated as the "Fifth Epistle" of Bishop Julius of Rome.

Basic to Apollinaris's picture of Christ is the "spirit-flesh" contrast found in Paul's letters. For Apollinaris, this contrast is understood as it applies to human nature. "Spirit" and "flesh" are parts of the human constitution, as in 1 Thess. 5:23. They refer to the intellect, or rational soul, and the body, the term "soul" being used in contrast to "intellect" or "spirit" and referring simply to the irrational, animal soul. Given this understanding of Paul's language, it was natural enough for Apollinaris to suppose that the incarnation of the Logos was like the embodiment of the rational soul in the case of a human being. The divine Logos "became human" in the sense that he became embodied and thus shared the structural constitution of a human being. He became an enfleshed intellect, though the intellect in question was not a created one. It was the divine original of created intellect, the Logos himself.

Apollinaris furthermore argues that there are good reasons for such a picture of Jesus. The doctrine that Jesus lacked a human intellect or rational soul seemed to him a matter of logical necessity. If the Logos had "put on" a rational soul as well as flesh, the result would, he thought, have been conflict. Either the Logos would simply dominate the human soul and thus destroy the freedom by which it was human, or the human soul would be an independent center of initiative and Jesus would be, in effect, schizophrenic. Much better to understand that the "human" intellect of Jesus was that of the model of humanity, the Logos. Moreover, this would help in understanding the saving virtue of the incarnation, for on this view the Logos himself becomes the life-principle of the flesh. Jesus' human body is governed and informed by the "life-giving spirit." For this reason it not only triumphs over sin and corruptibility itself but also becomes the transmitter of a divine quality of life to all who participate in it. It becomes the source of resurrected existence for all humanity and enables people to reconform themselves to the life of the one in whose image they were originally created.

Thus Apollinaris insists that Jesus is one, "one composite nature," in which flesh and divine intellect share the same life.

This unity means that even though the body truly is a body it is rightly spoken of as divine, and even though the Logos is truly God he is rightly spoken of as human. The human characteristics of Christ belong to the Logos, and the divine life is conferred on the body. There is, to use the later phrase, an "exchange" or "sharing" of properties: *communicatio idiomatum*. Apollinaris makes a great deal of this idea because it states the truth to which his christological outlook wants to point: that Christ simply is the divine Logos himself, but enfleshed. In this respect, of course, he is merely following lines of thought which Athanasius had also emphasized. Unlike Athanasius, however, he is clear and explicit in drawing out the consequences of his Logos-flesh model for the person of Christ. He does not forget or ignore a human center of life and consciousness in Jesus. He denies it.

Theodore of Mopsuestia

Needless to say, this Christology evoked strong criticism, and the strongest criticism of all came from a group of thinkers usually referred to as "the Antiochene school." To Apollinaris's idea of "one composite nature," they opposed the doctrine that there were "two natures" in Christ, the divine Logos on the one hand, and a complete human being, Jesus of Nazareth, on the other. This Antiochene tradition is often traced back to the third century, to the figure of one Paul of Samosata, who was condemned for teaching that Jesus was a human being inspired and indwelt by God. Certain it is, at any rate, that the fourth-century Antiochenes used this very model of "indwelling" to understand the nature of the incarnation—the model which Athanasius and Apollinaris were most eager to repudiate and which modern interpreters of patristic Christology have labeled the "Logos-Anthropos" model.

The reason for this appears twofold. For one thing, the Antiochenes generally were convinced that the sort of Christology represented by Apollinaris inevitably made the divine Logos the subject of human passions and debilities, and that as a matter of fact it entailed a change or corruption of the divine nature. Their answer to the Arian argument on this score was not, with Athanasius, that the Logos did hunger and thirst and suffer, though only "in the flesh." Their answer was rather that it was the human being who suffered and not the Logos at all. In consequence, they insisted on two subjects of attribution in Christ. Where Apollinaris spoke of "one hypostasis" (that is, one objective reality) and "one nature," the Antiochenes insisted that in Christ there were two hypostases and two natures.

This refusal to see the Logos as the subject of human limitations was not the only motive of the "two-nature" Christology of the Antiochenes. Equally important was another consideration. Athanasius and Apollinaris had at least one thing in common. They saw the divine Logos himself as the model of humanity, that image of God in which humanity was created. Accordingly, what was important to them was the identity of Jesus as the Logos, for they envisaged assimilation to the Logos as the proper destiny of a human being. In the Antiochenes, however, pious attention is focused rather on Jesus the human being in his struggle with evil. It was he, in his movement to a fulfilled life of immutable goodness, with whom they identified themselves and in whom they saw their own destiny realized. Therefore, their insistence on the full reality of Jesus' humanity grows out of their sense that redemption involves and issues in human moral activity, in conformity to God's law of goodness.

All these themes emerge in the christological writings of Theodore of Mopsuestia, the leading thinker among the Antiochenes. In his later years he was bishop of the small town of Mopsuestia in Cilicia, though most of his life was spent as a monk in Antioch. He died, some fifty years after Athanasius, on the eve of the Nestorian controversy (428). Because he was condemned by the Fifth Ecumenical Council (552), his doctrinal writings are available only in fragmentary form for the most part, but the fragments are numerous enough to provide a clear picture of his christological position.

At the basis of Theodore's Christology lies the image of divine "indwelling." He is aware, however, that this term describes a relationship between God and human beings which can be applied not only to the case of the incarnation but also to cases of what we may call "inspiration"—as with the prophets of the Old Testament, the apostles, or holy men and women generally. Accordingly, he argues that the incarnation represents a very special kind of indwelling, which makes it possible to speak of Jesus as a human being who truly shares the divine sonship of the Logos in a way that no prophet, apostle, or saint can. In Jesus, God dwells "as in a Son," he says. The Logos unites himself to Jesus from the moment of Jesus' conception, and as Jesus' human life goes on, maturing and fulfilling itself more and more through his struggle against evil, the reality of this union comes to fuller and fuller expression until, in the resurrection, the human being and the Logos show that they have always been, so to speak, one functional identity—one *prosōpon* or, to use the inadequate English equivalent, one "person." Thus Theodore teaches a "prosopic" union—a union which has its root in the fact that by God's gracious initiative this human life is perfectly at one, in its willing and acting, with the Logos.

The phrase "God's gracious initiative" needs emphasis. Theodore does not see the work of Christ as the product of a human initiative which God subsequently rewarded. It is God's doing—a genuine case of God's active presence with his people. The peculiarity of Theodore's teaching seems to lie in the fact that he conceives the relationship between God and humanity in the incarnation in terms of will rather than in terms of substance. God, he thinks, is present with or absent from people by the "disposition" of his will, by the way he attends to them. Thus the incarnation becomes a case of the Logos' gracious self-identification with a human being.

This means, of course, as we have said, that for Theodore and his followers, there are always two subjects in Christ. They express this belief by speaking indifferently of two "hypostases" (i.e., objective realities) or of two "natures." By the latter term they meant not two abstract essences but two concrete realities of different kinds. The divine "nature," for them, means the Logos, and the human "nature" means the man whom the Logos joined to himself. It was this dualism, this "two natures" doctrine, which made the Antiochene "Logos-Anthropos" model for the incarnation the subject of violent attack from the side of those who insisted that Jesus was, in the last resort, simply the Logos himself.

Cyril, Nestorius, and Eutyches

The disagreement between the proponents of Theodore's Christology and the defenders of the Athanasian-Apollinarian tradition came to a head in the second quarter of the fifth century. It took the form of a head-on collision between the sees of Constantinople and Alexandria and involved bitter political struggle as well as theological debate. It was resolved, at the behest of the Emperor Marcian, by the Council of Chalcedon (451), whose "Definition of Faith" became the standard of orthodox belief.

The debate may be said to have begun when Nestorius, an Antiochene monk and disciple of Theodore of Mopsuestia, became bishop of Constantinople in 428. A rash and dogmatic man, Nestorius quickly got himself in trouble with Cyril, the bishop of Alexandria. Not only did he foolishly permit himself to countenance accusations brought against Cyril by monks from Egypt, he preached, toward the end of his first year in office, a sermon attacking the view that the Virgin Mary is properly called *theotokos,* "mother of God," and suggesting that she be styled instead *theodochos,* "recipient of God." The underlying issue in this sermon was christological. In effect the question was whether it is proper to say that the divine Logos was born of a human mother—whether, in short, the Logos is the ultimate subject of the human attributes of Jesus. Nestorius's answer was no. It was, in his view, the human being Jesus who was in the proper sense born of Mary, just as it was the human being Jesus who suffered, died, and was raised. Nestorius's sermon was therefore an open challenge to the Christology of the Alexandrian tradition. It laid out the doctrine that Jesus is a human being who is intimately and completely indwelt by the Logos.

Cyril of Alexandria responded quickly. He exhorted Nestorius by letter to change his views. He denounced Nestorius to Pope

Celestine and rallied the Roman church behind him. In a series of writings—to his Egyptian monks, to members of the imperial family, and to Nestorius—he expounded the doctrine which he held to be the true one: that Jesus Christ is "one incarnate nature of the divine Logos."

This phrase Cyril had discovered in a work which was attributed to Athanasius but which in fact (unknown to him) had been written by Apollinaris of Laodicea. Cyril, however, was no Apollinarian. His writings from the period of the Nestorian controversy and after show that he affirmed the fullness of Jesus' human nature, its possession of soul as well as of body. What Cyril saw in this Apollinarian phrase was an affirmation of the view which, he insisted, was stated in the creed of the Council of Nicaea. The language of that creed makes it clear that the Logos, the divine Son, is the one who was born, suffered and died, and raised from the dead. As Cyril sees it, one must therefore affirm that Jesus is the Logos, but the Logos existing under the conditions of the human way of being—"incarnate." To make his point, Cyril dwells not only on the language of John 1:14 ("the Logos became flesh") but also on that of Phil. 2:5–11, which, as he understood it, showed the Logos "emptying himself" and taking on the "form" of human existence. This did not mean to Cyril—though Nestorius insisted it must mean so—that the divine Son underwent a change and so ceased to be God. On the contrary, it meant that while remaining God he took on, became the subject of, human life.

This position Cyril summed up by using the formula "union in hypostasis" or "hypostatic union." Nestorius thought that this phrase signified a kind of physical or chemical union of two substances—and therefore "mixture" or "confusion" in which the deity of Christ was altered and modified. In this understanding of Cyril, Nestorius was encouraged by the fact that Cyril had used the phrase "one nature" as an equivalent for "one hypostasis" and so seemed to deny the full reality of either the humanity or the deity of Christ. In fact, however, Cyril, in spite of certain ambiguities in his language, seems not to have meant this sort of thing at all.

27

"One hypostasis" and "one nature" were phrases which, for him, signified the fact that the humanity belonged so intimately to the Logos that there was actually only one subject or subsistent reality in Jesus. The one hypostasis and the one nature are the Logos himself, making a full human existence his own. They are not the "composite nature" that Apollinaris had taught.

The debate between Nestorius's christological dualism and Cyril's christological monism came to a head at the Council of Ephesus (431), where both sides were represented but met separately and mutually excommunicated each other. The imperial authorities, however, ultimately recognized the meeting over which Cyril had presided as the legitimate council; accordingly, Nestorius was sent into exile, his doctrine of "two sons" condemned as heretical. He himself continued his christological reflections and embodied them in a book which was only recovered in the late nineteenth century—*The Book of Heracleides of Damascus*. This prolix work develops his position in a more technical and careful way, but it played no part in the controversies of his time.

Cyril, for his part, announced himself glad to make peace with the supporters of Nestorius—the bishop of Antioch and the other bishops from the Eastern diocese of the Roman Empire. The peace was based on the so-called Formula of Reunion of A.D. 433, which Cyril quotes in his letter to John of Antioch confirming the reconciliation. In this document the Antiochenes concede the propriety of calling the Virgin Mary *theotokos*. At the same time, however, Cyril concedes the use of the expression "two natures" and agrees that one can distinguish attributes proper to Christ's humanity from attributes proper to his deity—it being affirmed at the same time of course that Jesus is Logos-made-flesh. This agreement cost Cyril credit with certain of his extreme supporters, but he maintained it until his death (444).

The original controversy was renewed in Constantinople in 448 as a result of the condemnation of a monk named Eutyches who taught that Christ had only "one nature after the union." An elderly and prominent archimandrite, Eutyches seems to have been a loyal, dogmatic—but ill-instructed—defender of the Alexan-

28

drian tradition. His case was nevertheless quickly taken up by Dioscorus, Cyril's nephew and successor as bishop of Alexandria. Dioscorus, with imperial support, presided over a council at Ephesus in August of 449 which restored Eutyches and deposed Flavian, the bishop of Constantinople, who had presided at the synod that condemned Eutyches.

Leo and Chalcedon

Before this action, Leo I ("the Great"), then head of the Roman church, had been brought into the conflict. Leo, in response to a report from Flavian, had sent a letter in June of 449 to Flavian condemning the teachings of Eutyches and accepting the action of the synod at Constantinople that had originally deposed him. In this *Tome,* as it is called, Leo set out the view of the person of Christ which had become traditional in the West. Using the language of Tertullian, Leo held that Christ was one "person" having two natures, each of which was the principle of a distinct mode of activity. To a traditional Alexandrian, his language would have seemed strongly dualistic, but the letter makes clear Leo's conviction that the inner, ontological identity of Christ is the Logos himself—a view which was the keystone of Cyril's position. This letter, together with the papal representatives who bore it, Dioscorus had refused to receive at his Ephesine council. Leo, therefore, labeling the council a "robber synod," insisted upon the authority of the Roman church and demanded another council to set matters right.

It was only with the death of Emperor Theodosius II and the accession of Marcian to the imperial throne in the East that Leo's demand was met. Marcian called a council to meet at Chalcedon, a city not far removed from the imperial capital at Constantinople. There, under the supervision of imperial commissioners, bishops from all over the East gathered, together with the representatives of the bishop of Rome. The council deposed Dioscorus almost immediately, but it had difficulty deciding what further actions to take. The Roman delegates were committed to the view that Leo's *Tome* was the authoritative, and hence decisive, document. The majority of the Eastern bishops, however, stood in the tradition of

Cyril of Alexandria and favored the position taken by his council at Ephesus in 431, which had affirmed that the creed of the Council of Nicaea (325) was sufficient for the determination of christological problems. The emperor, on the other hand, urgently desired a fresh pronouncement which would settle the christological debates that were dividing his subjects.

The product of these various pressures was a document which took careful account of all of them. The "Definition" of the Council of Chalcedon begins with an affirmation that the truth about the person of Christ and the mystery of redemption is satisfactorily stated in the creed of Nicaea as confirmed and expanded in the creed attributed to the Council of Constantinople of 381. It goes on, however, to explicit condemnation of Apollinarianism, Nestorianism, and Eutychianism—that is, to the extreme forms of both the Antiochene and Alexandrian christological traditions. As correctives to these heretical views, it proposes three documents: the *Tome* of Pope Leo, the second letter of Cyril to Nestorius, and Cyril's letter to John of Antioch accepting the Formula of Reunion of 433. These standards of orthodoxy are supplemented, finally, by a statement composed by the council itself in obedience to the wishes of the emperor.

This statement, which closes the "Definition," draws for its language on Cyril, Leo, and the Formula of Reunion. In Cyrillian style it emphasizes the unity of Christ. He is identified as the one divine Son, who possesses at once complete deity and complete humanity. At the same time, however, it insists not (with the Formula of Reunion) that Christ is "out of two natures" but that Christ exists "in two natures," which are neither divided from each other nor confused with each other. At the level of language, therefore, the "Definition" accepts the central emphases of both the Antiochene and the Alexandrian schools. Jesus Christ is "one hypostasis" but "in two natures," that is, he is a single reality, the divine Logos, existing as such, and at the same time existing as a human being.

This formula, the final product of the classical christological controversies, is essentially a rule of christological language. Its terms are not calculated to picture the way in which Jesus is put together. Rather, they are calculated to explain how it is proper to speak of him. Orthodoxy consists in the acknowledgment that Jesus is one subject, who is properly spoken of both as God—the divine Logos —and as a human being. To give an account of Jesus, then, one must talk in two ways simultaneously. One must account for all that he is and does by reference to the Logos of God, that is, one must identify him as God acting in our midst. At the same time, however, one must account for him as a human being in the ordinary sense of that term. Both accounts are necessary. One cannot understand Jesus correctly by taking either account independently, even while recognizing that they really are different accounts. There is a sense, therefore, in which it is true that the Council of Chalcedon solves the christological problem by laying out its terms. Its formula dictates not a Christology but formal outlines of an adequate christological language.

II.

Melito of Sardis

A HOMILY ON THE PASSOVER

(1) The passage dealing with the Hebrew Exodus has been read out and the words of the mystery have been explained: how the sheep is sacrificed and how the people is saved. (2) So then, my beloved friends, open your minds to understand. Here is the way in which the mystery of the Passover is new and old, eternal and involved in time, corruptible and incorruptible, mortal and immortal.

(3) It is old according to the Law, but new according to the Word. By being figure it is involved in time, but by being grace it is eternal. As the slaughter of a sheep it is corruptible; as the life of the Lord it is incorruptible. Because of the burial in the ground it is mortal, but because of the resurrection from the dead it is immortal. (4) The Law is old but the Word is new. The figure belongs to a particular time, but the grace is eternal. The sheep is corruptible, but the Lord is incorruptible. As lamb he is slaughtered, but as God he is risen. For though "like a sheep he was carried away to slaughter" [Isa. 53:7], yet he was no sheep; and though like a lamb he was "dumb," yet he was no lamb. For the one, the figure, was there, but the other, the reality, was uncovered.

(5) For in place of the lamb, God appeared, and in place of the sheep a human being, and within the human being, the Christ, who contains all things.

(6) So the slaughter of the sheep and the solemnity of the Passover and the scripture of the Law have arrived at Christ, for whose sake everything came to pass in the old Law, as it does all the more in the new Word. (7) For the Law became Word and the old, new

33

—issuing together out of Zion and Jerusalem. And the commandment became grace, and the figure became reality, and the lamb
became the Son, and the human being became God. (8) For as Son
he was born, as lamb he was carried off, as sheep he was slaughtered, as human being he was buried. He rose from the dead as
God, being by nature both God and a human being.

(9) He is everything: Law inasmuch as he judges, Logos inasmuch as he teaches, grace inasmuch as he saves, Father inasmuch
as he begets, Son inasmuch as he is begotten, sheep inasmuch as he
suffers, human inasmuch as he is buried, God inasmuch as he
rises. (10) This is Jesus the Christ, "to whom be glory to all the
ages. Amen."

(11) Such is the mystery of the Passover, as it is written in the
Law and as it was read just a moment ago. I will now review in
detail what the text says: how God gave a command to Moses in
Egypt when he wanted to bind Pharaoh by a plague while freeing
Israel from the plague by Moses' hand.

(12) "For behold," he says, "you shall take a faultless and un-
blemished lamb, and as evening comes you together with the sons
of Israel shall slaughter it, and at night you shall consume it in
haste and you shall break none of its bones" [Exod. 12:1ff.]. (13)
"This is what you shall do," he says. "You shall eat it in one night
gathered in families and in tribes. Your loins will be girded and
your staves shall be in your hands. For this is the Lord's Passover,
an eternal remembrance for the sons of Israel. (14) Then take the
blood of the sheep and smear the porches of your homes, placing
the sign of blood on the uprights of the entrance to deter the
angel. For behold, I smite Egypt; and in the space of one night,
she will be deprived of offspring, from beast to human being."
(15) Then when Moses had slaughtered the sheep and carried out
the mystery at night together with the sons of Israel, he sealed the
doors of their homes as a safeguard for the people and a deterrent
to the angel.

(16) So as the lamb is slaughtered and the Passover eaten and
the mystery accomplished and the people is glad and Israel sealed,
then the angel arrived to smite Egypt—Egypt uninitiated into the
mystery, having no part in the Passover, unsealed with the blood,

unprotected by the Spirit—this enemy, this unbelieving Egypt
(17) he smote and in one night deprived her of offspring. For when
the angel had passed about Israel and seen that the people were
sealed with the blood of the sheep, it came upon Egypt and tamed
the stiff-necked Pharaoh with sorrow, having put about him not a
garment of mourning or a mantle torn in shreds but the whole of
Egypt torn to pieces, sorrowing for her firstborn. (18) For the whole
of Egypt, in hardship and calamity, in tears and lamentations,
came all in mourning to Pharaoh—mourning not only in aspect,
but also in her soul, torn not only in outward vesture but also on
her delicate breasts. (19) There was a new spectacle to see: on the
one hand, people striking (themselves), on the other, people wailing; and in their midst a mourning Pharaoh, seated in sackcloth
and ashes, surrounded by a tangible darkness like funeral
garb—girded by all of Egypt, itself a cloak of mourning.

(20) For Egypt lay around Pharaoh like a vesture of mourning.
Such was the cloak which was woven for the tyrant's body. This is
the kind of garment in which the angel of justice dressed the harsh
Pharaoh: bitter mourning and tangible darkness and childlessness.
And the angel went on in its campaign against Egypt's firstborn,
for the death of the firstborn was rapid and tireless. (21) One could
see a new trophy raised up over those who had fallen dead in one
attack. And the ruin of those who lay about gave death something
to feed on. (22) And if you pay attention, you will discover a new
and unheard-of misfortune to marvel at. For look what enveloped
the Egyptians: a long night and tangible darkness, and death grop-
ing its way about, and an angel oppressing, and Hades devouring
their firstborn.

(23) But there is something yet stranger and more awesome for
you to hear. In this tangible darkness, death was hiding untouch-
able, and the unfortunate Egyptians probed the darkness; but
death, searching them out, touched the firstborn of the Egyptians
at the angel's order. (24) So if anyone probed the darkness, he was
led away by death.

If a firstborn child grasps a shadowy body with his hand, he cries
out pitiably and fearfully with fright in his soul, "Whom is my
hand holding? Whom is my soul afraid of? What darkness is it that

encompasses my whole body? If you be my father, help me! If my mother, share my pain! If my brother, address me! If my friend, be well-disposed! If my enemy, depart! For I am a firstborn." (25) But before the firstborn had fallen silent, the great silence seized him as it said, "You belong to me, firstborn. I, the silence of death, am your fate." (26) Another of the firstborn, observing that the firstborn were being taken, denied who he was, lest he die bitterly. "I am not a firstborn. I was born the third fruit of my mother's womb." But [the angel] could not be deceived. He seized the firstborn, who fell face down in silence. In one fell swoop the firstborn of the Egyptians perished. The first conceived, the firstborn, the desired one, the pampered one, was beaten to the ground—the firstborn not only of human beings but also of the irrational animals.

(27) On the fertile plains of the land there was heard a murmuring of beasts lamenting their nurslings, for the cow with a calf and the mare with a colt and the other beasts who were giving birth and swollen with milk were lamenting their firstborn offspring bitterly and pitiably. (28) There went up a wailing and a lamentation because of the destruction of the human [children], the dead firstborn. For the whole of Egypt stank because of the unburied corpses. (29) That was a fearsome sight to see: the mothers of the Egyptians with their hair in disarray, the fathers distracted, all wailing aloud terribly in their own speech, "In one fell swoop we unfortunates have been deprived of our children, even our firstborn offspring." And they beat their breasts, striking instruments with their hands as they did the dance of the dead.

(30) Such was the disaster which seized Egypt and rendered her childless in an instant. Israel, though, was protected by the sacrifice of the sheep and enlightened by the outpoured blood, and the death of the sheep was found to set a rampart around the people.

(31) O strange, unspeakable mystery! The sacrifice of the sheep was found to be Israel's salvation, and the death of the sheep became the life of the people, and the blood deterred the angel!

(32) Tell me, angel, what deterred you? Was it the sacrifice of the sheep or the life of the Lord? The death of the sheep or the prefiguration of the Lord? The blood of the sheep or the Spirit of the

Lord? (33) It is clear that you were deterred because you saw the mystery of the Lord coming to pass in the sheep, the life of the Lord in the sacrifice of the sheep, the prefiguration of the Lord in the death of the sheep. That is why you did not strike Israel, depriving only Egypt of children. (34) What is this unheard of mystery? Egypt was stricken for destruction, Israel was guarded for salvation.

Listen, and hear the power of the mystery. (35) The words [read], beloved, and the events which happen are unimportant apart from their character as parables and as preliminary sketches. Everything that happens and everything that is said has the quality of a parable. What is said has the quality of a parable, while what happens has that of an anticipation, in order that just as what happens is revealed by its anticipation, so also what is said is illuminated by the parable. (36) Except in the presence of a model, no work is accomplished. Or is not the coming reality perceived by means of the image which prefigures it? That is why the preliminary sketch of what is coming is made out of wax or clay or wood— so that the future accomplishment may be seen to be more exalted in height, and stronger in power, and beautiful in appearance and rich in its furnishing, by means of the littleness and corruptibility of the preliminary sketch. (37) When the thing to which the prefiguration points arrives, that which once bore the impress of what was coming is destroyed because it is no longer useful. The image has yielded to the truth it signified. What once was honorable becomes dishonorable, because that which is honorable by nature has appeared. (38) Each thing has its own moment. There is a time which belongs properly to the prefiguration, a time which belongs properly to the material. You construct the prefiguration of the truth. You desire it because in it you contemplate the image of what is coming. You bring up the materials before the prefiguration. You want this because of what will come to be by its means. You complete the work. You desire this alone, this alone you espouse, for in this alone you contemplate at once the prefiguration, the material, and the truth.

(39) As it is with the corruptible models, so it is with the incorruptible things. Just as it is with terrestrial things, so also it is with

37

heavenly things. For in the people is prefigured the Lord's salvation and truth, and the principles of the gospel are proclaimed beforehand by the Law. (40) Therefore the people became a prefiguration in a preliminary sketch, and the Law, the writing down of a figure. But the gospel is the Law's explanation and fullness, and the church is the receptacle of the truth. (41) So the type was honorable prior to the truth's coming, and the figure was astonishing prior to its interpretation. That is, the people was honorable before the church arose, and the Law was astonishing before the gospel was brought to light. (42) But when the church arose and the gospel stood forward, the type became an empty thing because it had handed its power over to the truth, and the Law was fulfilled because it had handed its power over to the gospel. Just as the prefiguration becomes an empty thing when it has handed its image over to the true reality so the parable becomes an empty thing when it has been illumined by its interpretation. (43) In the same way too the Law was fulfilled when the gospel had been brought to light, and the people was made an empty thing when the church had been raised up, and the prefiguration was destroyed when the Lord had been manifested. And today, what once was valued has become without value, now that things which are valuable in themselves have been revealed.

(44) For at one time the sacrifice of the sheep was a valuable thing, but now, because of the Lord's salvation, it is without value. The death of the sheep was valuable; but now, because of the Lord's salvation, it is without value. The blood of the sheep was valuable, but now, because of the Lord's Spirit, it is without value. The lamb which was dumb was valuable, but now, because of the spotless Son, it is without value. The temple here below was valuable, but now because of the Christ on high it is without value. (45) The Jerusalem here below was valuable, but now because of the Jerusalem on high it is without value. The narrow inheritance was once valuable, but now because of the broad grace it is without value. For the glory of God does not settle in one spot or within a narrow allotment of land. Rather, his grace is poured out to the limits of the inhabited world, and that is where the all-ruling God

has tabernacled, through Jesus Christ, to whom be glory to the ages. Amen.

(46) You have heard, then, the explanation of the prefiguration and of what corresponds to it. Hear also the shape of the mystery.

What is the Passover [Greek: *pascha*]? The name is taken from what in fact came to pass: "to keep Passover" [*paschein*] comes from the word "to have suffered" [*pathein*].

Learn, then, who it is who suffers and who shares his suffering, (47) and why the Lord is present on the earth—in order that, having garbed himself in the sufferer, he may carry him away into the heights of the heavens.

When "God in the beginning had made the heaven and the earth" [Gen. 1:1] and everything in them by the Logos, he molded the human being out of earth and shared breath with the form [he had made]. Then he set him in paradise, toward the East, in Eden, to live there contentedly. By a commandment he laid down this law: "Eat of every tree in paradise for nourishment, but do not eat of the tree of the knowledge of good and evil. On the day that you eat of it you shall die" [Gen. 2:16–17].

(48) But the human being, being naturally receptive to both good and evil, just as a parcel of soil is receptive to seed from either direction, took evil and gluttonous counsel; he touched the tree, he transgressed the commandment, and he disobeyed God. Therefore he was thrown out into this world as into a prison camp for the condemned. (49) When he had become prolific and very aged and had returned to the earth on account of his eating from the tree, he left an inheritance for his children. He left his children, as an inheritance, not chastity but adultery, not incorruption but corruption, not honor but dishonor, not liberty but slavery, not kingly rule but tyranny, not life but death, not salvation but perdition.

(50) The perdition of human beings on the earth was an unheard-of and frightening thing. Look what befell them: They were carried off by sin, their oppressor, and led into the world of lusts, where they were drowned by insatiable pleasures—adultery, fornication, impudence, lust, love of money, murders, bloodsheddings, the tyranny of evil, the tyranny of lawlessness. (51) For

39

father drew sword against son; and son lifted hand against father and, irreverent, struck his mother's breasts; and brother slew brother; and the host wronged his guest, and the friend murdered his friend; and human being slit the throat of his fellow with tyrannical hand. (52) So all the people on earth became murderers or fratricides or patricides or slayers of children. But something yet stranger and more fearful happened. A certain mother laid hands on the flesh to which she had given birth; she laid hands on those who had fed at her breast. She buried in her belly the fruit of her womb, and the ill-starred mother became a fearsome tomb, having devoured the child which she had borne. (53) I will say no more, but many other strange things, more fearsome and more wanton, came to pass among humans. A father lay with his daughter, and a son with his mother, and a brother with his sister, and a male with a male, and everyone lusted after his neighbor's wife.

(54) At this, sin was happy. Co-worker with death that she is, sin made her way first into people's souls and got the bodies of the dead ready for death to feed on. Sin left her mark in every soul, and those in whom she left it were those who had to come to an end. (55) So all flesh fell under sin, and every body fell under death, and every soul was removed from its fleshly home, and what had been taken from earth was resolved into earth, and what had been given by God was closed up into Hades, and the happy union was dissolved, and the beautiful body was broken up into parts. (56) Humanity was being cut in parts by death, for a new kind of misfortune and captivity held it. It was carried away captive under the shadow of death. The image of the Father was left desolate. This, then, is the reason why the mystery of the Passover has been completed in the body of the Lord. (57) The Lord, however, laid out the order of his own sufferings ahead of time in the persons of the patriarchs and the prophets and the People as a whole, and set his seal to it through the Law and the Prophets. For since the future will be both unprecedented and grand, it was arranged ahead of time from afar, so that when it came to pass it would encounter faith because it had been foreseen. (58) In this way the mystery of the Lord, prefigured from afar and made visible today, encounters faith now that it is accomplished, even though people judge it to

be something novel. The mystery of the Lord is both new and old, old inasfar as it is prefiguration, new inasfar as it is grace. But if you gaze steadily upon this prefiguration, you will see the reality by way of its fulfillment.

(59) So if you want to see the mystery of the Lord, gaze upon Abel who was similarly murdered, Isaac who was similarly bound, Joseph who was similarly sold for slavery, Moses who was similarly exposed, David who was similarly persecuted, the prophets who similarly suffered on account of the Christ. (60) Gaze also upon the sheep sacrificed in the land of Egypt and the one who smote Egypt and saved Israel by means of blood.

(61) Furthermore, the mystery of the Lord is proclaimed by the prophetic voice. For Moses says to the people, "And you will see your life hanging before your eyes by night and by day, and you will not believe in your life" [Deut. 28:66]. (62) David, for his part, said, "Why were the nations troubled, and why did the peoples concern themselves with empty things? The kings of the earth stood there and the rulers were gathered together against the Lord and against his Christ" [Ps. 2:1–2]. (63) Then Jeremiah said, "I am like an innocent lamb led to slaughter. They contrive evil against me, saying, 'Come, let us cast wood into his bread and throw him out of the land of the living, and his name will never be remembered'" [Jer. 11:19]. (64) Then Isaiah said, "Like a sheep he was led to slaughter and like a speechless lamb before his shearer he does not open his mouth. Who can recount his generation?" [Isa. 53:7–8]. (65) Many other things too were proclaimed by many prophets with reference to the mystery of the Passover, which is Christ, "to whom be glory to the ages. Amen."

(66) He arrived on earth from the heavens for the sake of the one who suffered. He clothed himself in the sufferer by means of a virgin's womb and came forth as a human being. He took to himself the sufferings of the sufferer by means of a body capable of suffering, and he destroyed the sufferings of the flesh. By a Spirit incapable of death he killed off death, the homicide.

(67) This is the one who like a lamb was carried off and like a sheep was sacrificed. He redeemed us from slavery to the cosmos as from the land of Egypt and loosed us from slavery to the devil as

41

from the hand of Pharaoh. And he sealed our souls with his own Spirit and the limbs of our body with his own blood. (68) This is the one who covered death with shame and made a mourner of the devil, just as Moses did Pharaoh. This is the one who struck lawlessness a blow and made injustice childless, as Moses did Egypt. This is the one who rescued us from slavery into liberty, from darkness into light, from death into life, from a tyranny into an eternal kingdom [and made us a new priesthood and a peculiar, eternal people].

(69) He is the Passover of our salvation. He is the one who in many folk bore many things. He is the one who was murdered in the person of Abel, bound in the person of Isaac, exiled in the person of Jacob, sold in the person of Joseph, exposed in the person of Moses, sacrificed in the person of the lamb, persecuted in the person of David, dishonored in the person of the prophets. (70) This is the one who was made flesh in a virgin, hanged upon the wood, entombed in the earth, raised from the dead, lifted up to the heights of the heavens. (71) He is the speechless lamb. He is the lamb who was slaughtered. He is the one born of Mary the beautiful ewe. He is the one who was taken from the flock and dragged to slaughter and killed at evening and buried at night, who was not crushed on the cross, was not dissolved into the earth, who rose from the dead and raised humanity from the grave below.

(72) This man was killed. And where was he killed? In the middle of Jerusalem. And why? Because he cured their lame and cleansed their lepers and led their blind to sight and raised up their dead. That is why he suffered. Somewhere it is written in the Law and the Prophets: "They have rendered me evil for good and repaid my soul with childlessness. They reckoned evil against me and said, 'Let us bind the just man, for he is of no use to us'" [Ps. 34:14 LXX].

(73) Why, O Israel, did you do this new misdeed? You dishonored the one who honored you. You have held in low esteem the one who esteemed you. You have denied the one who confessed you. You have renounced the one who publicly called out your name. You have done to death the one who gave you life. What have you done, O Israel? (74) Has it not been written for

your sake, "You shall not shed innocent blood, lest you die miserably" [Jer. 22:6]?

"I," says Israel, "slew the Lord. Why? Because he was bound to suffer." You have gone astray, Israel, in using such sophistry to deal with the Lord's sacrifice. (75) He had to suffer, but not because of you. He had to be dishonored, but not by you. He had to be judged, but not by you. He had to be hanged, but not by your hand. (76) These, O Israel, are the words with which you ought to have called to God: "O Master, if indeed your Son must suffer and this is your will, let him suffer, but not because of me; let him suffer at the hands of other nations. Let him be judged by the uncircumcised. Let him be crucified by the hand of a tyrant, but not by mine."

(77) This, however, is not what you called out to God, O Israel. Nor did you make atonement before the Lord. You have not been put to shame by the sight of his works. (78) The withered hand restored for the sake of its body's well-being did not shame you, nor did the eyes of infirm folk opened by his hand, nor did paralyzed bodies restored by his voice. Neither did the most novel of all shame you—when a dead person was raised from the tomb after four days. You, in fact, passed these things by. On the eve of the Lord's sacrifice you prepared sharp nails and false witnesses and bonds and scourges and sour wine and gall and a sword and calamity, as though for a murderous robber. (79) When you had laid scourges to his body and thorns on his head, you bound his good hands, which had formed you out of earth, and fed with gall that good mouth which had fed you with life, and you did your Lord to death on the great feast. (80) And you dined cheerfully while he went hungry. You drank wine and ate bread while he had vinegar and gall. You ate with beaming face while he was of melancholy countenance. You were rejoicing, but he suffered affliction. You sang songs, but he was condemned. You were beating time, but he was being nailed up. You were dancing, but he was being buried. You stretched out on a soft couch, but he was in a grave and in a coffin.

(81) O wicked Israel, why did you carry out this fresh deed of injustice, bringing new sufferings upon your Lord—your master,

your creator, your maker, the one who honored you, who called you Israel? (82) But you were discovered not to be Israel, for you have not seen God or acknowledged the Lord. You did not know, O Israel, that this one is God's firstborn, who was generated before the morning star, who made light to come up, who made the daylight gleam, who set the darkness to one side, who established the first limit, who suspended the earth, who dried up the abyss, who stretched out the firmament, who set the cosmos in order, (83) who arranged the stars in heaven, who made the lights gleam, who created the angels in heaven, who fixed the thrones there, who molded humanity upon the earth.

It was this one who called you and guided you, from Adam to Noah, from Noah to Abraham, from Abraham to Isaac and Jacob and the twelve patriarchs. (84) It was this one who led you into Egypt and protected you and there nourished and nursed you. It was this one who gave you light by means of a pillar of fire and sheltered you by means of a cloud, who cut open the Red Sea and led you through and scattered your enemies abroad. (85) It was this one who rained manna on you from heaven, who gave you drink from a rock, who gave you the Law on Horeb, who gave you an inheritance on earth, who sent you the prophets, who raised up your kings. (86) This is the one who came to you, who cured those of you who were suffering and raised up your dead. This is the one whom you treated impiously. This is the one whom you treated unjustly. This is the one whom you put to death. This is the one on whom you set a price in money, after demanding from him didrachmas for his head.

(87) Come, ungrateful Israel, be judged before my face for your ingratitude.

What value have you set on his guiding you? What value have you set on his election of your fathers? What value have you set on the descent into Egypt and your being nourished there by that good man Joseph? (88) What value have you set on the ten plagues? What value have you set on the pillar by night and the cloud by day and the crossing of the Red Sea? What value have you set on the gift of manna from heaven and the possession of water from the rock and the giving of the Law on Horeb and the earthly inheritance and the gifts you received there? (89) What value have you set on the sufferers whom he cured when he was with you? Set me a value on the withered hand which he restored to its body. (90) Set me a value on those blind from birth to whom he brought light by his voice. Set me a value on the dead ones whom he raised from the tomb after three or four days.

His gifts to you cannot be measured. You, however, without honoring him, have repaid him with ingratitude. You have repaid him evil for good and affliction for joy and death for life— (91) to him on whose account you ought to have died.

For if the king of a nation is seized by its enemies, for his sake war is begun, for his sake a wall is breached, for his sake a city is taken, for his sake ransoms are sent, for his sake ambassadors are dispatched, so that he may be taken—either in order that he may be restored to his life or in order that, being dead, he may be buried.

(92) You, on the contrary, voted against your Lord. The nations worshiped him. The uncircumcised marveled at him. The out-landers glorified him. Even Pilate washed his hands in this case. This one you did to death on the great feast.

(93) So for you the Feast of Unleavened Bread is bitter, as it is written, "You will eat unleavened bread with bitter herbs." Bitter for you the nails which you sharpened. Bitter for you the tongue which you sharpened. Bitter for you the false witnesses which you set up. Bitter for you the bonds which you prepared. Bitter for you the whips which you plaited. Bitter for you Judas whom you re-warded. Bitter for you Herod whom you obeyed. Bitter for you Caiaphas in whom you trusted. Bitter for you the gall which you furnished. Bitter for you the vinegar which you produced. Bitter for you the thorns which you gathered. Bitter for you the hands which you stained with blood.

You did your Lord to death in the midst of Jerusalem.

(94) Listen and see, all families of the nations! An unprece-dented murder has come to pass in the midst of Jerusalem, in the city of the Law, in the Hebrew city, in the prophets' city, in the city adjudged righteous. And who has been killed? Who is the killer? I am ashamed to say and compelled to speak. If the murder took

place by night, or if he was slaughtered in a desert place, to be silent were an easy matter. But it was in the midst of street and city, in the midst of a city of onlookers, that the unjust murder of a just man took place. (95) And so he was lifted up upon a tree and an inscription was provided too, to indicate who was being killed. Who was it? It is a heavy thing to say, and a most fearful thing to refrain from saying. But listen, as you tremble in the face of him on whose account the earth trembled. (96) He who hung the earth in place is hanged. He who fixed the heavens in place is fixed in place. He who made all things fast is made fast on the tree. The Master is insulted. God is murdered. The King of Israel is destroyed by an Israelite hand.

(97) O unheard of murder, O unheard of injustice! The Master, his body naked, has had his appearance altered, and he is not even deemed worthy of a garment to keep him from being seen. That is why the stars turned aside in their courses and the daylight was obscured, so as to conceal him who was stripped naked on the Tree —not obscuring the Lord's body, but the eyes of these people. (98) Though the people did not tremble, the earth trembled. Though the people were not afraid, the heavens were afraid. Though the people did not rend their garments, the angel did. Though the people did not wail and lament, "The Lord thundered from heaven and the Most High gave forth his voice" [Ps. 18:13].

(99) That is why, Israel, you did not tremble before the Lord, you did not fear before the Lord, you did not lament over the Lord, you gave vent to grief over your own firstborn. When the Lord was hanged, you did not rend your garments, but for your own when they had been murdered you rent your garments. You deserted the Lord, you were not found by him. You cast the Lord down, you were cast down to earth. And you—you lie dead, (100) while he rose from the dead and went up to the heights of heaven.

The Lord, when he had put on the human being and suffered for the sake of him who suffered and was bound for the sake of him who was imprisoned and was judged for the sake of the condemned and was buried for the sake of the buried, (101) rose from the dead and cried aloud, "Who will enter into judgment against me? Let him stand up and face me. I have set the condemned free.

I have given the dead life. I have raised up the one who was entombed. (102) Who will speak against me? I,'' he says, "the Christ, I have dissolved death, I have triumphed over the enemy and trodden down Hades and bound the strong man and carried off humanity into the height of the heavens—I,'' he says, "the Christ.''

(103) "So come, all families of human beings who are defiled by sins, and receive remission of sins. For I am your remission, I am the Passover of salvation. I am the Lamb sacrificed for your sake. I am your ransom. I am your life. I am your resurrection. I am your light. I am your salvation. I am your King. I lead you toward the heights of heaven. I will show you the eternal Father. I will raise you up with my right hand.''

(104) This is he who made the heavens and the earth, and formed humanity in the beginning, who is announced by the Law and the Prophets, who was enfleshed in a Virgin, who was hanged on the Tree, who was buried in the earth, who was raised from the dead and went up into the heights of heaven, who is sitting on the right hand of the Father, who has the authority to judge and save all things, through whom the Father made the things which exist, from the beginning to all the ages. (105) This one is "the Alpha and the Omega,'' this one is "the beginning and the end''—the beginning which cannot be explained and the end which cannot be grasped. This one is the Christ. This one is the King. This one is Jesus. This one is the Leader. This one is the Lord. This one is he who has risen from the dead. This one is he who sits on the right hand of the Father. He bears the Father and is borne by the Father. "To him be the glory and the power to the ends of the ages. Amen.''

Peace to him who wrote and to him who reads and to those who love the Lord in simplicity of heart.

III.

Irenaeus of Lyon

AGAINST HERESIES

Book III   Chapter 18

(1) It is now plain from the evidence that the Logos who "existed in the beginning with God," "through whom everything was made," and who has always been humanity's companion is the one who, in the last days, at the moment preordained by the Father, was united to the creature he had shaped, and became a human being subject to hurt. Consequently, there is no place for the objection of those who say, "If the Christ was born at that moment, then he did not exist prior to it." We have shown that, since he has always existed with the Father, he did not begin to be God's Son at that particular point. Nevertheless, when he was enfleshed and became a human being, he summed up in himself the long history of the human race and so furnished us with salvation in a short and summary way, to the end that what we had lost in Adam (namely, to be after the image and the likeness of God) we might recover in Christ Jesus.

(2) It was impossible that the very humanity which had once been conquered and shattered by its disobedience should reconstitute itself and obtain the prize which belongs to victory. Furthermore, it was impossible for a humanity which had fallen under the domination of sin to lay hold on salvation. Therefore, the Son accomplished both things. Existing as God's Logos, he descended from the Father and became enfleshed and humbled himself to the point of death and completed God's program for our salvation. Paul again exhorts us to believe in this without doubting, and he

says, "Do not say in your heart, 'Who ascends into heaven?' (that is, to bring Christ down) or 'Who descends into the abyss?' (that is, to free Christ from the dead)" [Rom. 10:6–7]. Then he adds, "For if you confess with your mouth that Jesus is Lord and believe in your heart that God raised him from the dead, you will be saved" [Rom. 10:9]. Further, he explains why God's Logos did these things. He says, "To this end Christ both lived and died and was raised, so that he might be Lord of the living and the dead" [Rom. 14:9]. And again, writing to the Corinthians, he says, "But we proclaim Christ Jesus crucified" [1 Cor. 1:23], and adds, "The cup of the blessing which we bless, is it not a sharing in the blood of Christ?" [1 Cor. 10:16].

(3) Who is it, though, who shares nourishment with us? Is it the Christ they make up for themselves, "the Christ from on high" who "is stretched out over *Horos*" (that is, "limit") and who gave shape to their mother? Or is it Emmanuel, who was born of a virgin and "ate butter and honey," of whom the prophet said, "Yes, he is a human being, and who shall know him?" [Jer. 17:9]. Paul proclaims precisely the same person. He says, "For I handed over to you in the first place that Christ died for our sins according to the Scriptures, and that he was buried, and rose on the third day according to the Scriptures" [1 Cor. 15:3–4].

So it is obvious that Paul did not know of any Christ other than the one who suffered and was buried and rose and was also born, the one whom he also calls a human being. For after he says, "But if Christ is proclaimed as one raised from the dead" [1 Cor. 15:12], he adds an account of the reason for the Christ's becoming flesh. "Since," he writes, "death came through a human person, resurrection from the dead also comes through a human person" [1 Cor. 15:21].

What is more, he invariably uses the name "Christ" in connection with our Lord's suffering and his humanity and his being put to death. For example, there is the case of the words "Do not destroy with your food the one for whom Christ died" [Rom: 14:5] and "Now, however, you who were once far away have been brought near in the blood of Christ" [Eph. 2:13] and "Christ redeemed us from the curse of the Law by being made a curse for our sake, for it is written, 'Cursed is everyone who hangs on the tree'" [Gal. 3:13] and "On account of your knowledge, the weak one will perish, the brother on whose account Christ died" [1 Cor. 8:11].

The point is that there is no Christ incapable of suffering who came down upon Jesus. On the contrary, Christ himself suffered on our behalf because he was Jesus Christ, the one who died and rose, who descended and ascended—the Son of God become Son of man. This, after all, is what the word itself means. By the name "Christ" is connoted one who anoints, the one who is anointed, and the ointment itself with which he is anointed. Now, in point of fact, the Father has anointed, but the Son has been anointed— in the Spirit who is the ointment. That is why the Logos says through Isaiah, "The Spirit of God is upon me because he has anointed me" [Isa. 61:1], referring at once to the anointing Father, the anointed Son, and the ointment, which is the Spirit.

(4) What is more, the Lord himself makes it plain who it was that suffered. When he had asked his disciples, "Who do people say that the Son of man is?" [Matt. 16:13ff.], and when Peter had answered, "You are the Christ, the Son of the living God," and when he had commended Peter "because flesh and blood did not reveal it to him, but the Father who is in heaven," he made it clear that this "Son of man" is "the Christ, the Son of the living God." "For," the text says, "from that moment he began to show his disciples that he must go to Jersualem and suffer many things from the priests, and be rejected and crucified, and rise again on the third day." The very man whom Peter recognized as the Christ, and who called Peter "blessed" because the Father had revealed to him the Son of the living God, insists that he himself must suffer many things and be crucified. Furthermore, he then rebuked Peter, who understood him to be Christ in the popular sense of that term and [so] repudiated his suffering. And he said to his disciples, "If anyone wants to come after me, let him deny himself and take up his own cross and follow me. For anyone who wants to save his life shall lose it, and anyone who loses it on my account

51

shall save it" [Matt. 16:24–25]. Christ used to say this publicly, since he himself was the savior of those who would be given over to death and lose their lives because of their confession of him.

(5) If it was not the Christ himself who was going to suffer—if, on the contrary, he "flew away" from Jesus—why did he exhort his followers to carry the cross and follow him when, on the Gnostic account, he himself did not carry it but rejected suffering as a part of his work? When he spoke these words he was not talking about getting to know some "heavenly cross," as certain people have the audacity to explain this text. What he meant was the suffering which he had to undergo, and the fact that the disciples themselves would also suffer. That is why he added, "Whoever saves his life will lose it, and whoever loses his life will find it." Furthermore, he told the Jews that his disciples were going to suffer on his account: "Behold, I send prophets and wise men and teachers to you, and of their number you will kill and crucify some" [Matt. 23:34]. He said also to the disciples, "Before leaders and kings will you stand on my account, and some of you they will flog and kill and chase from town to town" [Matt. 10:17–18]. So he knew those of his disciples who would suffer persecution, and also those who would have to be flogged and killed on his account. What is more, he was talking not about some different, some alternative, cross, but about the suffering which first he, and then his disciples, would undergo.

That is why his word also exhorts them, "Do not be afraid of those who kill the body but cannot kill the soul, but fear him rather who has the power to send both soul and body into Gehenna" [Matt. 10:28]—and to hold fast by their confessions of faith concerning him. He promised that he would confess before the Father those who should confess his name before men, and that he would deny those who denied him, and that he would be ashamed of those who were ashamed of their confession of him.

And in spite of the fact that this is the case, these people have the boldness and the rashness to scorn even the martyrs and to disparage those who get killed because of their confession of the Lord and who put up with all the things foretold by the Lord and who, in this fashion, try to follow the way of his suffering as witnesses to the sufferer. For our part we refer these critics to the martyrs themselves, for when "answer is made for their blood" [Luke 11:50] and they attain glory, then all who have dishonored their witnessing will be put to confusion by Christ.

By the fact that on the cross the Lord said, "Father, let them go, for they do not know what they are doing," the long-suffering and patience and mercy and goodness of Christ are shown, so that the very one who suffers is the one who forgives his persecutors. The word of God which he spoke to us—"Love your enemies and pray for those who hate you" [Matt. 5:44]—he enacted on the cross. He loved the human race so much that he interceded for those who were doing him to death.

If there is anyone who thinks that there were two Christs and passes judgment on them, he will discover that the Christ who, in spite of his own wounds and stripes and the other things they did to him, was beneficent and willing to forget the evil done him, was much better and more patient and truly good than the Christ who "flew away" and did not suffer injury or opprobrium.

(6) This consideration also supplies the answer to those who say that Christ suffered in appearance only. If he did not really suffer, it is no credit to him, since there was no passion. And where we are concerned, when we begin actually to suffer he will seem a deceiver as he exhorts us to get ourselves beaten and to turn the other cheek, if he did not first suffer in the same way himself. Just as he led his disciples astray by seeming to be something he was not, so he leads us astray too by exhorting us to put up with things he did not put up with. What is more, we will be greater than our teacher inasmuch as we suffer and bear things which our teacher neither suffered nor bore.

But as our Lord is the only true teacher, he is also the true Son of God, who is good and who suffers in patience—the Logos of God the Father become Son of man. He struggled and conquered. He was a human being, fighting on behalf of his fathers. Through his obedience he dissolved disobedience, for he tied up the strong man and set free the weak. He gave salvation to the being he had shaped by destroying sin. He is the most faithful and merciful Lord and the lover of the human race.

(7) Therefore, as I have said, he caused humanity to cleave to God—he united humanity with God. For if a human person had not conquered humanity's foe, that foe would not have been conquered justly. Conversely, unless it was God who conferred salvation, we should not possess it securely, and unless humanity had been closely united to God, it could not have become a sharer in incorruptibility. It was necessary that "the mediator between God and human beings" [1 Tim. 2:5], through his sharing in the life of both, bring the two together in friendship and harmony and bring it about both that humanity is made over to God and that God is made known to human beings.

On what basis could we be sharers in adoption as God's sons? We had to receive, through the Son's agency, participation in him. The Word, having been made flesh, had to share himself with us. That is why he went through every stage of human life, restoring to all of them communion with God.

Consequently, those who say that he was manifested only in appearance, and that he was not born in the flesh and did not truly become a human person, are still under the ancient condemnation, they still lend their support to sin. As they see it, death is not conquered, which "reigned from Adam to Moses, even in those who did not sin in the way Adam did" [Rom. 5:14].

But the Law came, which was given through Moses, and bore witness about sin to the effect that it is a sinner. The Law deprived sin of its rule, showing it up as a thief and not a king and revealing it to be a man-killer. Yet the Law put a great burden on the person who had sin within himself, by showing that he was legally liable to death. For even though the Law was of the Spirit, all it accomplished was to show up sin; it did not slay it. Why? Because sin was ruling not over the Spirit but over the human race.

So it was necessary that the agency which was to kill sin off and to release humanity from its liability to death should become exactly what that humanity was—a human being who had been carried off into slavery by sin and was held in thrall by death—so that sin might be slain by a human being and humanity escape from death.

Just as "through the disobedience of one human person," the

very first to be shaped out of untouched earth, "the great mass of people became sinners" and lost their hold on life, so also it was necessary that "the mass of people be justified" and receive salvation "through the obedience of one human person" [Rom. 5:19], the first to be born of a virgin. The Logos of God therefore became a human being just as Moses said, "God—true are his works" [Deut. 32:4]. But if, without being made flesh, he appeared to be flesh, his work was not true. In fact, however, he was as he appeared: God recapitulating in himself the age-old shaping of the human creature, so that he might kill off sin, be rid of death, and give life to humanity; and because this is so, "true are his works."

Chapter 19

(1) Those who say he was born from Joseph as nothing more than an ordinary human being are in process of dying, for they are persisting in the enslavement which belongs to the original disobedience. They are not yet in a relationship of sharing with the Logos of God the Father, nor are they recipients of the liberty which comes through the Son, as he himself says, "If the Son releases you, you will really be free" [John 8:36]. Being ignorant, moreover, of that Emmanuel who is born of a virgin, they are deprived of his gift, which is eternal life. Since they are not recipients of the Logos who is incorruption, they continue in the mortality of the flesh. They are liable to death since they do not take in its remedy, which is life.

It is to people of this sort that the Logos, telling of his own gift of grace, says, "I have declared that you shall all be sons of the Most High and gods, but you are dying like human beings" [Ps. 82:6–7]. Without question he is addressing these words to those who do not receive the gift of adoption but on the contrary despise the incarnation constituted by the unstained birth of God's Logos. They cheat humanity of advancement toward God, and they are ungrateful to the Logos of God, who became incarnate on their account. The Logos of God became a human being, and the Son of God was made Son of man, so that humanity, having received the Logos and accepted adoption, might become Son of God. The only way in which we could receive incorruption and immortality was by being united with them. But how could we be united with incorruption and immortality unless first of all they became what we are, so that "the corruptible might be swallowed up by incorruption and the mortal by immortality" [1 Cor. 15:53-54] and so we might receive adoption as sons?

(2) That is why Scripture asks, "Who will tell of his birth?" [Isa. 53:8] since "he is a human being, and who will know him?" [Jer. 17:9]. But the person who knows him is the person "to whom the heavenly Father has revealed him" [Matt. 16:17]—in order that it may be understood that this person, who "is born not of the will of the flesh nor of the will of the male" [John 1:13], is Son of man, that is, Christ the Son of the living God. We have already shown from the Scriptures that not one of the sons of Adam is called "god" in the proper sense of the term, or named "lord." It is, however, possible for all who have grasped even a fragment of the truth to see that, above all the human beings of his time, this one was proclaimed, at once by the prophets, the apostles, and the Spirit himself, to be in the proper sense God and Lord and King eternal and Logos incarnate. The Scriptures, however, would not have testified so about him if, like everyone else, he had been a mere human being. But since, in contrast to everyone else, he possessed that glorious birth which is from the most high Father, and since he also made his own the birth from a virgin, the divine Scriptures testify two things about him at the same time: on the one hand, that he was not a comely person, was subject to suffering, rode on the foal of an ass, drank vinegar and gall, was despised among the people, and humbled himself to the point of death; and, on the other hand, that he is Holy Lord, Wonderful, Counselor, and beautiful to look upon, and mighty God, and Judge of all who comes on the clouds. All this the Scriptures prophesy of him.

(3) Just as he was a human being in order that he might be tempted, so too he was the Logos in order that he might be glorified. On the one hand, the Logos became quiescent so that he could be tempted and be dishonored and be crucified and die; on the other hand, the human being was taken up by the Logos in his

56

conquering and enduring and rising and being received on high. Therefore he, the Son of God, our Lord, and the Father's Logos, and also Son of man because he was born of Mary (who came of the human race and was herself a human being), was born in human fashion and became Son of man.

For this reason "the Lord himself gave us a sign . . . in the depth and again on high" [Isa. 7:14, 11]. It was a sign no one ever asked for, for no one ever hoped that a virgin would become pregnant, managing while a virgin to give birth to a son, or that this offspring should be "God with us." He "descended into the lower parts of the earth" [Isa. 7:14] to "search for the sheep which was lost" [Luke 15:4-6], the creature which he himself had shaped. He ascended on high, bearing and commending to the Father that humanity which he had sought out, and creating in his own person the firstfruits of humanity's resurrection. He did this so that just as the Head rose from among the dead, so also the rest of the body— every human being who is found in life—will, when the time of the condemnation brought upon it by sin has been completed, rise also. It will grow together through its joints and structures, given strength by the increase which God gives it, and in this body each member will have its own appropriate place, for there are many dwellings in God's presence, there being also many members in the body.

Book V   Chapter 1

(1) We could not learn the things of God unless our teacher, already existing as God's Logos, became a human being. For one thing, no one could interpret for us the mysteries of the Father save his very own Logos. "Who" else "knows the mind" of the Father save his very own Logos? "Who" else "knows the mind of the Lord? Or who" else "has become his counselor" [Rom. 11:34]? Moreover, we could not learn the things of God unless, by seeing our teacher and hearing his voice for ourselves, we became imitators of his deeds and doers of his words. In that way we have communion with him. As persons recreated, we receive growth at the hand of one who is perfect and who exists prior to the whole creation. By

the agency of him who alone is perfectly excellent and good and who has the gift of incorruptibility, we are established in his likeness. Indeed, when we did not yet exist, we were predestined to exist in accordance with the Father's foreknowledge and were created at a time fixed beforehand by the ministry of the Logos, who is perfect in every way because he is both powerful Logos and true human being. It is he who redeemed us by his own blood in a way suited to his character as Logos and "gave himself as a ransom" [1 Tim. 2:6] for those who had been taken captive.

Furthermore, by reason of the fact that the apostate power, by making us his own pupils, oppressed us unjustly and alienated us in a way contrary to nature (for by nature we belong to almighty God), the Logos of God, powerful in every way and unfailing in justice, acted justly even in opposing that same apostate power. He redeemed his own from it, not by violence (which is the way that power got control of us to begin with: it snatched insatiably at what did not belong to it) but by persuasion, for that is the proper way for a God who persuades and does not compel in order to get what he wants. Consequently, justice was not infringed, and neither did the creature which God had shaped of old perish.

Since it is true, then, that the Lord redeems us by his own blood, that he gives his life for our life and his flesh for our flesh, that he pours out the Spirit of the Father to unite God and humanity and bring them into communion, bringing God down to human beings through the Spirit and, conversely, bringing humanity up to God by his own incarnation, and that, futhermore, he truly and securely gives us incorruptibility at his coming by creating communion with God—since all this is true, the teachings of the heretics are destroyed.

(2) The people who assert that his appearance was a matter of mere seeming speak emptily, for these things did not seem to happen, they *did* happen, in objective reality. If he appeared to be a human being when he was not, then as Spirit of God he did not truly continue to be what he was, since the Spirit is invisible; nor was there any truth in him, since he was not what he appeared to be. We have said already that Abraham and the rest of the pro-

phets saw him prophetically, declaring on the basis of a vision what was going to happen. If, therefore, he appears even now in this fashion, and is not what he appears to be, what has happened is that some prophetic vision has come to people. We must then await yet another advent for him, one in which he will be what prophecy now sees him to be.

We have shown that it is one and the same thing to say that his appearance was a matter of mere seeming and to say that he took nothing from Mary. He would not have had the true flesh and blood through which he redeemed us unless he had recapitulated in himself the ancient formation of Adam. So the followers of Valentinus speak emptily when they lay these teachings down as authoritative so that they may rule out the salvation of the flesh and denigrate God's formation.

(3) The Ebionites also speak vainly. They do not, through faith, receive into their souls the union of God and humanity. Rather, they continue in the old leaven of the birth they now have. Moreover, they choose not to understand that the Holy Spirit came upon Mary and that the power of the Most High overshadowed her, for which reason what was born [of her] was something holy and was in fact the Son of the most high God [cf. Luke 1:35], the Father of all, who effected the Son's incarnation and manifested a new birth, with the intent that as we inherited death through our previous birth, so we might inherit life through this one.

Thus these people repudiate the mixing of heavenly wine [in the chalice at the Eucharist]. They want only the water which the present order of things supplies, and do not accept God into their mixture. So they continue in the Adam who was conquered and thrown out of paradise. They do not see that just as, from the very beginning of our shaping in Adam, the breath of life from God gave life to humanity because it was united to the work which God had shaped, so also, in the end, God's Logos and God's Spirit, united to the ancient substance [produced by] Adam's formation, have brought about a living and completed humanity which embraces God in his completeness—all of which means that as, in the order of ordinary life, we have died, so in the spiritual order we are all made alive. Adam never escaped those hands of God which the Father addresses when he says, "Let us make humanity after our image and likeness" [Gen. 1:26]. That is why, at the end, it was not "by the will of the flesh, or by the will of a male" but by the good pleasure of the Father, that his hands completed a living humanity so that Adam might come to be after the image and likeness of God.

IV.

Tertullian

AGAINST PRAXEAS

Chapter 27

Why, though, do I delay over such obvious matters when I ought to be tackling the arguments in which they attempt to take the obvious and obscure it? At every point they are put to silence by the fact that a distinction is made between Father and Son—a distinction which, since the two continue to be joined together, we explain as one between the sun and its ray or a fountain and the stream [which flows from it].

In spite of this, however, they take up the idea of an undivided composite of two and three elements, and they attempt to interpret the distinction [between Father and Son] in another fashion, one consonant with their views. What it amounts to is that they conveniently distinguish the two things—Father and Son—within one person. They say that the Son is the flesh (i.e., the human being—Jesus) while the Father is the Spirit (i.e., God—the Christ). So those who argue that Father and Son are one and the same now start dividing them rather than identifying them! If Jesus is one thing and Christ another, the Son will be different from the Father, since the Son is Jesus and the Father is Christ. This kind of "monarchy"—which makes two different things out of Jesus and Christ—they must have learned from Valentinus.

The force of this proposal of theirs is, however, already blunted by what we have just shown—that what they refer to as "Father" is called "Word of God" or "Spirit of God and power of the Most High." For things which are said to belong to the Father are not identified with him; rather, they are said to be from him or of him. But these people will find further refutation, of a different sort, in this chapter.

They call attention to the message of the angel: "Therefore what will be born will be called holy, the Son of God" [Luke 1:35]. Since it is flesh which gets born, it will be flesh which is the Son of God. That is wrong, though. The reference is to the Spirit of God, for it is certain that the Virgin conceived "of Spirit," and what she conceived is what she bore. Consequently, what had been conceived and was coming to birth is what had to be born—that is, Spirit, whose name is "Emmanuel, which means 'God with us' "[Matt. 1:23]. Flesh after all is not God, and so it cannot be said of flesh that "it will be called holy, the Son of God." The reference there is to the God who has been born in the flesh, of whom the psalm says, "For God has been born in her as a human being and has built her up by the will of the Father" [Ps. 87:5]. What God is this who "has been born in her"? The Word, and the Spirit, who with the Word has been born of the Father's will. Therefore it is the Word who is enfleshed.

But there is a question. In what way did the Word become flesh? Was it transformed into flesh, or did it put on flesh? Obviously it put on flesh. One must in any case suppose that God is immutable and not susceptible to having his being shaped for him. This follows from his being eternal. But transformation means the destruction of what was there originally, for everything that is transformed into something else ceases to be what it was and begins to be what it was not. God, however, does not cease to be [what he is], nor can he become something different. Moreover, the Word is God, and the Word of the Lord endures forever, persisting, that is, in his form. If he is not capable of conformation to something else, it follows that he must be understood to have become flesh in the sense that he comes to be within flesh and is manifested and seen and touched through flesh, for there are also other reasons that demand this interpretation.

If the Word became flesh by way of transformation and change of substance, the result will be a single substance of Jesus made out of two substances, flesh and Spirit. Some composite will result, like electrum out of gold and silver, and he will begin to be neither gold (that is, Spirit) nor silver (that is, flesh), since in fact each is altered by the other and a *tertium quid* is produced. Therefore Jesus will not be God, for the Word which has been made flesh has ceased to be; nor will the human being be flesh, for the flesh does not, strictly speaking, exist, seeing that it was [once] the Word. Thus out of both things you have neither. The *tertium quid* is far different from both.

Yet we discover that he is explicitly set before us both as God and as a human being. The very psalm we are discussing suggests it: "For God has been born in her as a human being and has built her up by the will of the Father." Certainly we discover that he is everywhere set before us as Son of God and Son of man. This follows from the fact that he is, without a shadow of doubt, proposed to us as God and a human being with the differing properties of each substance, for "Word" means nothing else than "God," and "flesh" means nothing else but "human being." The apostle, too, teaches in this way about the duality of substance. He writes, "who came to be of the seed of David" (this will mean the human being and the Son of man), and then "who was shown to be the Son of God according to the Spirit" [Rom. 1:3–4] (this will mean God and the Word of God, his Son). What we see here is two ways of being, not compounded but conjoined, in one person, Jesus, who is God and a human being. (I put off discussion of the title "Christ.") The characteristic property of each substance is preserved in so real a way that the Spirit carried on its own activities in him—that is, powers and works and signs—and at the same time the flesh was involved in its passions, hungering in his encounter with Satan, thirsting in his meeting with the Samaritan woman, weeping over Lazarus, disturbed to the point of death, and at length dead. If, though, it were a question of some *tertium quid* compounded out of both substances, like electrum, such distinct indications of the duality of substance would not appear. Rather, the Spirit would have engaged in fleshly activities and the flesh in spiritual activities, by an exchange; or else, as a result of compounding, neither fleshly nor spiritual activities would have been carried out, but activities of some third

63

sort. Obviously either the Word would have died, or the flesh would not have died, if the Word had been turned into flesh, for either the flesh would have been immortal or the Word, mortal. Since, however, each substance acted distinctly in its own way of being, it followed that what came to each was the deeds and the destiny which were proper to it.

Learn, therefore, with Nicodemus that what is born in the flesh is flesh, and what is born of the Spirit is Spirit. Neither does flesh become Spirit, nor Spirit, flesh; and so they can, plainly, be together in one [person]. These are the things of which Jesus was constituted, human by reason of the flesh and divine by reason of the Spirit. The angel at his appearance pronounced him Son of God in virtue of that side of his nature by which he was Spirit, reserving "Son of man" for the flesh. So too the apostle, in calling him a mediator of God and men [1 Tim. 2:5] confirms the twofold substance.

Finally, you who say that "Son of God" means "flesh," show us who the Son of man is. Surely it will not be the Spirit. But you want to take "Spirit" to mean the Father himself on the ground that the Spirit is God—as if God's Word were not also Spirit of God, just as the Word is God.

ON THE FLESH OF CHRIST
Chapter 1

(1) Those who are so driven to disturb people's belief in the resurrection—a belief which stood without controversy before the appearance of this lot of near Sadducees—as to maintain that the hope of the resurrection does not extend to the flesh are well advised to aim their destructive questions at the flesh of Christ too, to assert either that it did not exist at all or that in some fashion it was more than human. Otherwise, if it were a settled matter that his flesh was human, there would be a presumption, contrary to their position, that flesh does indeed rise again, since it has risen in the case of Christ. Consequently, it will be our business to defend the prospects of the flesh at the very point where these people set out to tear them down.

(2) Let us look closely at the Lord's corporeal substance, for the question of his spiritual substance is settled. It is to his flesh that people pose questions. They ask whether it is real and what its quality is. They want to know whether it existed and where it came from and what sort of thing it was. Its reply will determine what resurrection means for us.

Marcion, in order to deny Christ's flesh, denied his birth also, or else he denied the flesh in order to deny the birth. Obviously, he was afraid that birth and flesh might bear witness to each other, since there is no birth apart from flesh or flesh apart from birth. . . .

Chapter 3

(1) To the extent that you [Marcion] consider yourself competent to judge in this matter, you must have thought either that birth is *impossible* for God or that it is *unsuitable* for him.

For God, however, nothing is impossible save that which he does not choose. So let us consider the question whether he chose not to be born (for if he did choose it, he was both able to do it and was in very fact born).

I descend to a summary argument: If God had chosen not to be born, for whatever reason, then neither would he have allowed himself to appear as a human being, for who, seeing him to be a human being, would deny that he was born? God would certainly not have chosen to appear as what he had chosen not to be.

(2) People reject even the appearance of something which displeases them, for it is not important whether something exists or not if it is presumed to exist even though it does not. What obviously is important is that God should not suffer deceptively what he is not in reality. "But," you say, "his own self-awareness was sufficient for him. It was people's own fault if they thought him born because they saw he was human."

(3) How much more worthily, therefore, and self-consistently he might have faced people's conviction of his humanity it he really was born—when, even if he were not, he would face the same conviction on their part, and with injury done to his self-awareness. What sort of trustworthiness do you call it if, when he was not born he let people think he was, in opposition to his own self-

knowledge? Tell me, why was it such a good thing for Christ to pass himself off for what he was not when he knew what he was?

(4) You cannot say, "If he had been born, and had truly clothed himself in humanity, he would have ceased to be God, he would have lost what he was in the process of becoming what he was not"; for God is in no danger of losing his nature. "But," you say, "the reason I deny that God was turned into a human being in such wise as to be born and embodied in flesh is that he who has no end cannot be changed, for when something is changed into something else, the original reality comes to an end. (5) Change into something else, therefore, is unfitting in the case of something for which it is unfitting to come to an end."

It is true that the nature of changeable things is that they do not persist in that aspect of their character which is undergoing change. Thus, since they do not persist they perish, for by the process of being changed they lose what they have been. But nothing is in the same case as God. His nature is far removed from the state of all existing things. So if things which are far removed from God and from which God is far removed lose what they were in the process of being changed, where will the difference be between deity and other natures, unless it is that the contrary obtains, that is, that God is able both to change into everything and yet to continue such as he is? (6) Otherwise, God will be on a level with things which, when they have been changed, lose what they have been. But God is not on a level with them in any respect and so he cannot be on a level with them with respect to the result of his changing.

You have read at one time or another, and believed, that the Creator's angels have been changed into the appearance of a human being and that their bodies were real enough both for Abraham to have washed their feet and for Lot to be rescued from the Sodomites by their hands. Also, an angel wrestled with a human being with all the strength of his body and requested that human being, who was holding him down, to release him. (7) What was permitted to the angels of the inferior God, when they had been changed into the solidity of the human body—namely, to remain angels in spite of it—you deny to God, who is more powerful, as if his Christ were unable truly to put on humanity and still remain God. Or did those angels appear as phantoms of flesh? This you will never dare to assert, for if you were to allow that the Creator's angels are in the same situation as Christ, he would turn out to be the Christ of that same God whose angels share his condition.

(8) If you had not busily rejected some and corrupted others of the Scriptures which oppose your view, the Gospel of John would have refuted you in this matter. It declares that the Spirit came down in the body of a dove and settled upon the Lord. When the Spirit was in this state, it was just as truly dove as it was Spirit; nor had the alien substance which it took on destroyed its own proper substance.

(9) But you ask, "Where is the dove's body now that the Spirit has been taken back into heaven?" The case is like that of the angels' bodies. It was taken away in the same fashion as that in which it had been put forth. If you had been a witness when it was being brought out of nothing, you would have known also when it was being reduced to nothing. If it had no visible beginning, then it had no visible end either. At whatever time the body was seen, though, it was solid as a body is. What is written must have been the case.

Chapter 4

(1) So then, if it is neither as impossible nor as dangerous to God that you repudiate his becoming embodied, it remains for you to reject and denounce it on the ground that it is unworthy of him.

Come, then, start from birth itself, the object of aversion, and run through your catalog: the filth of the generative seeds within the womb, of the bodily fluid and the blood; the loathsome, curdled lump of flesh which has to be fed for nine months off this same muck. Describe the womb—expanding daily, heavy, troubled, uneasy even in sleep, torn between the impulses of fastidious distaste and those of excessive hunger. Then, too, inveigh against the modesty of the woman who is giving birth, a modesty to be honored because of the danger it involves or counted holy because of its nature.

(2) Undoubtedly you are also horrified at the infant, which has

67

been brought into the world together with its afterbirth. Naturally, too, you disdain it when it is washed, when it is dressed in swaddling clothes, when it is cleaned up with oil and mocked with blandishments. You repudiate such veneration of nature, do you, Marcion? Well, but how were *you* born? You hate a human being in process of birth? In what possible way can you love anyone? Plainly you did not love yourself when you departed from Christ's church and from faith in him. But let it be your own problem if you displease yourself or if you were born in some other fashion.

(3) Christ loved that human being, that lump curdled in the womb in the midst of impurities, that creature brought into the world through unmentionable organs, that child nourished on mockery. On his account Christ came down. On his account Christ preached. On his account Christ, in all humility, brought himself down to death, the death on a cross. Clearly he loved one whom he redeemed at great cost. If Christ belongs to the Creator, then it was his own creation he loved—rightly. If he is from some other God, he loved the more greatly for the fact that what he redeemed was not his own. Together with the human being, therefore, he loved the human being's birth as well—even his flesh.

Nothing can be loved apart from that in virtue of which it is what it is. (4) If you think otherwise, take the birth away and show me the human being. Remove the flesh and bring forward the one whom God redeemed. If these things are part of the human being whom God redeemed, will you render what he redeemed shameful to him? He would not have redeemed what he did not love. Will you make it something demeaning to him? By a heavenly rebirth he remakes our birth, putting death away. He restores our flesh so that it is free from trouble; he cleanses it when leprous, gives sight to it when blind, heals it when paralyzed, purifies it when it is demon-possessed, raises it when it has died. Does he then blush to be born in it?

(5) Suppose that in point of fact he had wanted to be born of a wolf or a ewe or a cow and put on the body of some animal, wild or domestic, to proclaim the kingdom of heaven. In that case, I judge, your censure of him would say, "This is unseemly for God and unworthy of God's Son, and anyone who believes it is a fool."

To be sure, it is foolish if we judge God on the basis of our own understanding. But look around, Marcion, if you have not cut the text out: "God chose the foolish things of the world to confound the wise" [1 Cor. 1:27].

(6) What are these "foolish things"? People's conversion to worship of the true God? The rejection of error? The training in justice, modesty, mercy, patience, and innocence? Surely these are not "foolish." Ask yourself what he was referring to, even though you think you have already found out. What is so "foolish" as to believe in a God who has been born—and of a virgin at that, and in fleshy form too—and who has wallowed about in those very degradations of nature? (7) Perhaps someone says that these are not the "foolish things," and perhaps it is the case that there are other things which God has chosen for the sake of surpassing the wisdom of this age. Yet that wisdom more easily believes that Jupiter became a bull or a swan than Marcion does that Christ truly became man.

Chapter 5

(1) What is more, there obviously are other things that qualify as foolish—those related to God's reproaches and sufferings. Marcion, either label a crucified God "good sense" or strike out this episode too—this one above all! What is more demeaning to God, what is more shameful—getting born or dying? To carry flesh or to carry a cross? To be circumcised or to be hanged? To be fed at the breast or to be buried? To be laid in a manger or shut up in a tomb? It would be wiser for you not to believe these things either. But you will not be wise unless, by believing God's "foolish things," you have been foolish in this age.

(2) Or is your reason for not cutting out Christ's sufferings the fact that he is a phantom and free from the experience of them? We have previously said that he could have undergone the empty mockery of imaginary birth and infancy. But answer me this, you murderer of truth: Was not God truly crucified? And being truly crucified, did he not truly die? And having truly died, was he not truly raised? (3) Was it falsely that Paul determined to know among us only one who had been crucified? Did he falsely present

69

him as buried? Did he falsely teach that he had been raised? In that case, our faith is false too, and everything we have hoped from Christ is a deceit.

Most evil of men, why do you excuse the murderers of the Lord? From them Christ suffered nothing if in truth he did not suffer at all. Spare the one hope of the whole world! Why do you destroy the indispensable disgrace of the faith? What is unworthy of God is needful for me. I am saved, if I am not ashamed of my Lord. He says, "If anyone is ashamed of me, I will also be ashamed of him" [Matt. 10:33]. (4) There is no other ground for shame which I can find that will establish me, by my scorn for blushing, as one who is utterly shameless and happily foolish. The Son of God has been crucified; the fact evokes no shame because it is shameful. Furthermore, the Son of God died; the fact can be believed because it makes no sense. Furthermore, he rose from the dead after burial; the fact is certain because it is impossible.

(5) In what way will these things hold true of [Christ] if he himself was not true, if he did not truly have what it takes to be crucified, to die, to be buried, and to be raised—that is, this flesh of ours, suffused with blood, built up on bones, woven through with sinews, intertwined with veins? Flesh which knew how to be born and to die, flesh which was indubitably human because born of a human being and therefore mortal—this is what, in Christ, will be taken as "humanity" and "Son of man."

(6) Else why, if there is nothing human about him, nothing derived from a human being, is Christ [called] "human being" and "Son of man"? It would have to be the case, Marcion, either that a human being is something other than flesh, or that human flesh is derived elsewhere than from a human being, or that Mary was something other than a human being, or that Marcion's God is a human being. Except on these conditions, Christ will not be termed "human being" in the absence of flesh or "Son of man" in the absence of any human parent, just as he will not be called "God" apart from divine Spirit or "Son of God" apart from God the Father.

(7) Thus the recorded activity of the twofold substance has shown him to be both a human being and God. In virtue of the

one he was born; in virtue of the other, unborn. In virtue of the one he was fleshly; in virtue of the other, spiritual. In virtue of the one he was feeble; in virtue of the other, mighty. In virtue of the one he was dying; in virtue of the other, alive. The special quality of the two ways of being—divine and human—is settled and established by the equal reality of each nature, both the Spirit and the flesh. With the same trustworthiness, the mighty works of God's Spirit establish that he is God, and his suffering shows that he is human flesh. (8) If there are no mighty acts apart from the Spirit, by the same token there are no sufferings apart from the flesh. If the flesh with its sufferings is a fraud, so too the Spirit with its mighty acts is a deceit. Why do you divide Christ in half with your lie? He was the truth in his completeness. Believe it. He preferred being born to being a liar in either of his capacities.

Chapter 10

(1) I turn to another group, equally clever in their own eyes. They assert that the flesh of Christ is composed of soul-stuff, on the ground that it was soul which was made flesh. The consequence [of this view] is not only that the soul is flesh but also that the soul is fleshly just as the flesh has the qualities of soul.

In this case, too, I want to know the reasons [for the assertion].

Grant that Christ took soul into himself in order to bring salvation to the soul, because it could only be saved by him if he made it his own. I do not see why he made it into flesh by putting on a flesh with the qualities of soul, as though he could not find a means of bringing salvation to the soul save by making it fleshly. (2) After all, he brings salvation to our souls, and they are not only not fleshly but quite disparate from flesh. How much more, then, could he save the very soul which he assumed, even though it was not fleshly!

Further, they presuppose that Christ came forth not to liberate the flesh but solely to liberate our soul. On this hypothesis, how absurd it is, in the first place, that when he was going to liberate only the soul he should have made it into the very sort of body he was not going to liberate! (3) In the second place, if he undertook to liberate our souls through the medium of the soul which he

71

bore, then that soul of his ought to have borne whatever ours does—that is, it ought to have been of the same form as ours. And whatever is the form of our soul in its secret nature, it is not that of flesh. Besides, he did not liberate our soul, if he had a fleshly soul, for ours is not fleshly.

V.

Origen

ON FIRST PRINCIPLES
Book II   Chapter 6

(1) Now that we have dealt with these matters, the time has come to return to the subject of the incarnation of our Lord and Savior: in what way and for what reason he was made a human being. To the extent of our modest abilities, we have inquired about the divine nature, more on the basis of God's works than on that of our own understanding of him. We have also, with equal care, contemplated his visible creations and likewise, by faith, his invisible creations. (For human weakness is such that it cannot either perceive everything with the eyes or grasp everything by reason, seeing that we human beings are, among the totality of rational beings, the animal which is most feeble and weakest. The beings found in heaven or above the heavens are superior.) So it remains for us to seek the mean, that is, the mediator, between all these creatures and God, whom the apostle Paul announces as the firstborn of the whole created order.

We are aware, too, of what the Scriptures say about his majesty, and we realize that he is called "the image of the invisible God and firstborn of the whole created order" and that "in him all things have been created, visible and invisible, whether thrones or dominions or principalities or powers: all things have been created through him and in him, and he is before all, and all things hold together in him" [Col. 1:15–17], who is the head of all things, having only God the Father for his own head (for it is written: "The head of Christ is God" [1 Cor. 11:3]). Also, we clearly see it

73

written that "no one knows the Father except the Son, nor does anyone know the Son except the Father" [Matt. 11:27], for who can know what Wisdom is except the one who gave birth to her? Or who knows clearly what truth is except the Father of truth? Who is able with certainty to find out the total nature of the Logos of God, the God who comes from God, except God alone, with whom the Logos existed [cf. John 1:1]. So we take it as established that no other except the Father alone knows this Logos—or perhaps we should say Reason—this Wisdom, this Truth, of which it is written, "I doubt if the world itself would contain the books which would be written" [John 21:25]—that is, about the glory and the majesty of the Son of God. For it is impossible to write down the things that pertain to the Savior's glory.

Consequently, when we have taken account of all these facts about the nature of God's Son, we are numbed with wonder at the fact that this nature, higher than all, emptied itself of its condition of majesty and became a human being and lived among human beings—just as "the grace spread out on his lips" [Ps. 45:2] testifies, just as the heavenly Father bears witness to him, and just as the signs and wonders and various mighty acts which he performed establish. Even before this presence of his which he made apparent through a body, he sent the prophets as precursors and heralds of his arrival; and after his ascension into the heavens, he caused his holy apostles to go about into the whole world—men filled with the power of his divinity, drawn now from among tax collectors, now from among ignorant and unskilled fishermen—in order to gather together, from every race and all nations, a people who faithfully believe in him.

(2) But of the whole number of miracles and marvels attributed to him, there is one which exceeds the capacity of the human mind for admiration, and which the weakness of mortal understanding can find no way to grasp or to compass. I mean the fact that that great power of majesty divine, the very Logos of the Father as well as the very Wisdom of God, in whom all things visible and invisible were created, must be believed to have been circumscribed within the human being who appeared in Judaea; and what is more, that the Wisdom of God must be believed to have entered a

woman's womb, to have been born as a small child, and to have squalled in the manner of crying children.

In addition, it is reported that he was troubled in the face of death, as he confesses himself when he says, "My soul is sad even to the point of death" [Matt. 26:38, cf. Mark 14:34], and that in the end he was brought to that form of death which we consider the most demeaning, though he rose from the dead after the third day. Since, therefore, we see in him qualities so human that they stand in no way apart from the common weakness of mortals, and qualities so divine that they befit nothing except that highest and ineffable nature which is deity, the human intellect is seized with perplexity and so silenced with amazement that it cannot tell where to go, what to think, or where to turn. If it discerns God, what it sees is a mortal. If it thinks him a human being, what it perceives is one returning from the dead bearing the spoils of death's conquered empire.

Consequently, we must gaze upon him with thorough fear and reverence, to the end that in one and the same [subject] the reality of a twofold nature may be so exhibited [to us] that on the one hand we attribute nothing unworthy or unfitting to that divine and ineffable essence, while on the other hand we make no judgment that the actions and deeds are an illusion produced by deceptive appearances. Obviously, to set all this forth for people and explain it in speech far exceeds the power at once of our deservings, our talents, and our words. I judge, however, that it surpassed the capacity of even the holy apostles; indeed, when all is said, the explanation of this mystery may reach even beyond the whole created order of the heavenly powers. On this subject, accordingly, because the structure of this book demands it, and not out of rashness, we set forth, in the fewest possible words, the content of our faith rather than the ordinary deliverances of human reason, and we offer our suppositions rather than obvious assertions.

(3) So then, the Only Begotten of God—through whom, as our earlier argument taught, "all things have been created, visible and invisible" [Col. 1:16]—both made all things, as the Scriptures testify, and loves what he has made. Since he is himself the invisible "image of the invisible God" [Col. 1:15], he conferred invisibly a

participation in himself upon all rational creatures. He did this in such a way that each received from him a degree of participation proportioned to the degree to which it clung to him with a disposition of love. But since the capacity for free choice belonged to each of the intellects, each was characterized by variety and diversity, and therefore one was possessed by a more burning love for its author, while another's love was thinner and weaker.

But that soul of which Jesus said, "No man will take my soul from me" [John 10:18], that soul, from the beginning of its creation and after, clung inseparably and persistently to him, to the Wisdom and Logos of God, the truth and the true light. It received, as a whole, the whole [of the Logos]. It entered itself into his light and his glory. So it was made, in the proper sense, one spirit with him—just as the apostle promises, to those called to imitate this soul, that one "who joins himself to the Lord is one spirit" [1 Cor. 6:17].

Therefore, with the reality of this soul to mediate between God and flesh—for it was not possible for the divine nature to be mingled with body apart from a mediator—God, as we have said, was born a human being; he had, as an intermediary, this substance for which assuming a body was not something that went against its nature. Conversely, however, inasmuch as that soul was a rational substance, neither was it contrary to its nature to be receptive of God; as we stated above, it had already entered into God in God's character as Logos and Wisdom and complete truth. Consequently, in view of the fact that it existed totally in God's Son, or else received God's Son wholly into itself, that very soul, together with the flesh which it had assumed, is correctly called Son of God and Power of God, Christ, and Wisdom of God. Conversely, the Son of God, through whom all things were created, is named Jesus Christ and Son of Man. For the Son of God is said to have died, by virtue, to be sure, of the nature which is truly capable of sustaining death. At the same time he is called the Son of man, who is announced to be coming in the glory of God the Father with the holy angels. This is the reason why, throughout the Holy Scriptures, the divine nature is as frequently described by means of terms that suit the human condition as the human nature is honored by titles ordinarily applied to God. It can be said in this case more appropriately than in any other that "the two will be in one flesh, and they are no longer two but one flesh" [Gen. 2:24]. We are bound to suppose that the Logos of God is more truly "in one flesh" with the soul [of Jesus] than a man is with his wife. Furthermore, for whom is it more appropriate to be "one spirit" with God than for this soul, which so joined itself to God by love that it is deservedly called "one spirit" with him?

(4) So perfection in love and integrity in a praiseworthy disposition have created for that soul this inseparable unity with God. Therefore, God's assumption of that soul was not a chance affair nor a case of favoritism. Rather, it was accorded to that soul by reason of the merit of its virtues. This is what we hear as the prophet addresses this very soul: "You have loved justice and you have hated iniquity. Therefore God, your God, has anointed you with the oil of gladness beyond those who share with you" [Ps. 45:7]. This implies that it is for the sake of its love that it is anointed with the oil of gladness—or, in other words, that the soul of Christ together with the Logos of God is constituted the anointed one, for to be anointed "with the oil of gladness" is nothing other than to be filled with the Holy Spirit. Furthermore, what the expression "beyond those who share with you" points to is not the fact that this soul is given this grace of the Spirit in the manner of the prophets but the fact that the substantive fullness of the very Logos of God dwelt within it, as the apostle said: "In whom the whole fullness of the deity dwelt bodily" [Col. 2:9].

This is why the prophet not only said, "You have loved justice," but also added, "and you have hated iniquity." Hatred of iniquity is what Scripture ascribes to him in the words "He did no sin, and no guile was found in his mouth" [Isa. 53:9] and again in the words "Tempted in all things by reason of his likeness, without sin" [Heb. 4:15]. Furthermore, the Lord himself says, "Which of you accuses me of sin?" [John 8:46]. Again he himself says of himself, "Behold, the prince of this world is coming and in me he finds nothing" [John 14:30]. All these texts point to the fact that in Christ there existed no sense of sin. To emphasize more plainly that a sense of sin never entered into him, the prophet said, "Before the boy knew how to call his father or his mother, he turned himself away from iniquity" [Isa. 7:16; 8:4].

(5) There may well seem to be a difficulty here, growing out of the fact that, as we have shown above, there is a rational soul in Christ. In all our investigations we have frequently demonstrated that it is natural for souls to be capable of both good and evil. The difficulty in this case will be explained in the following manner.

There can be no doubt that the nature of Christ's soul was that which belongs to all souls. If it had not in fact been a soul, it could not even be called by that name. Since, however, the capacity to choose good and evil is present in all souls, this soul, which belongs to Christ, chose to love justice in such a way that justice was rooted unchangeably and inseparably within it, in proportion to its immeasurable love. Consequently, firmness of intent and depth of attachment and warmth of inextinguishable love set aside any possibility of a knowledge of change and alteration. Furthermore, what had its location in choice has by now, through the attachment created by long habit, become a matter of nature. Thus it is true both that we must believe Christ to have had a human and rational soul and that we must judge him to have had neither sense nor possibility of sin.

(6) For the sake of a fuller explanation of this matter, however, it does not seem out of place to employ an analogy, even though in a matter so hard and difficult it is not even within our power to find appropriate illustrations. Nevertheless—to speak apart from any consideration of this difficulty—iron is receptive to both cold and heat. Think, then, of a certain quantity of iron which is kept always in a fire. It takes in fire by all its pores and passages. It is entirely made into fire.

If the fire never for a moment leaves it, and it is not removed from the fire, what happens? Can we possibly assert that this, which by its nature is plainly a quantity of iron, can at some point take on the quality of being cold when it has been located in a fire and is burning away incessantly? On the contrary, we say what is closer to the truth, that (just as we have frequently seen it happen in furnaces with our own eyes) this iron has been completely turned into fire, on the ground that nothing is seen in it save fire, and, what is more, that anyone who tried to touch or handle it would feel the effect not of iron but of fire. In this fashion, therefore, that soul which, like the iron in the fire, has been abidingly placed in the Logos, in Wisdom, in God, is God in all its acting, all its feeling, and all its understanding. Consequently, it cannot be called changeable or mutable. It possesses unchangeability because it is unceasingly fired by its unity with God's Logos.

We must, of course, suppose that some of the heat of God's Logos has made its way to all holy people, but we are bound to believe that the divine fire itself came to rest on this soul in its full reality, and that it is by derivation from this source that a portion of heat has reached the others.

Finally, the text "God, your God, has anointed you with the oil of gladness beyond those who share with you" shows that this soul is anointed with "the oil of gladness" (that is, God's Logos and Wisdom) in a fashion different from that in which "those who share with" it (that is, the holy prophets and apostles) are anointed. The latter are said to have run "to the smell of his perfumes" [Song of Sol. 1:3], but this soul was the jar which contained the ointment itself, and the prophets and apostles were made worthy of sharing in the fragrance it gives off. Therefore, just as the ointment itself is one thing and its perfume another, so Christ is one thing and those who share with him are another. By the same token, just as the very jar which contains the ointment cannot possibly acquire an unpleasing smell, while those who share in its perfume can, if they get too far away from its fragrance, acquire a stench which blots it out, so Christ, being the jar itself which contains the real ointment, could not possibly acquire another smell, while those who share with him will participate in, and have a capacity for, his perfume in proportion to their nearness to the jar which gives it off.

(7) It is my opinion that the prophet Jeremiah too understood the nature of the divine Wisdom which was in Christ, as well as the nature of the soul which he had assumed for the salvation of the world; that is why he said, "The Spirit of our countenance is the Lord Christ, to whom we have said that we will live among the nations in his shadow" [Lam. 4:20]. Consider the fact that the

shadow of our body is inseparable from the body itself. It takes over and carries out the body's movements and gestures without alteration. I think that Jeremiah wanted to indicate the operation and activity of Christ's soul, which clung inseparable to the Logos and did everything according to his motion and will, and so he referred to the soul as the "shadow" of "the Lord Christ," in which "we live among the nations." The nations live in the mystery of the taking-on of this soul [by the Logos]. As they imitate it through faith they come to salvation.

David seems to me to suggest the same sort of thing when he writes "Be mindful, O Lord, of the reproach with which they insult me in the place of your anointed one" [Ps. 89:50–51]. And what else is it that Paul realizes when he says, "Your life is hidden with God in Christ" [Col. 3:3]? It is true that he says, in another place, "Do you seek a proof of the Christ who speaks in me?" [2 Cor. 13:3]; and here he says that Christ is "hidden in God." If the point of this text is not the same as that which the prophet conveys, as I said above, by his reference to the "shadow" of Christ, perhaps it goes beyond any meaning the human mind can grasp. We do, however, find a multitude of other references to shadows in Scripture, as for example in Luke's Gospel when Gabriel says to Mary, "The Spirit of the Lord will come upon you, and the Power of the Most High will overshadow you" [Luke 1:35]. Moreover, the apostle says regarding the Law that those who have a fleshly circumcision "serve a likeness and a shadow of the heavenly things" [Heb. 8:5]. And elsewhere it is said, "Is not our life a shadow upon the earth" [cf. Job 8:9]. So then the Law, which is "upon the earth," is a shadow, and our whole life, which is "upon the earth" is a shadow, and we "live among the nations" in the shadow of Christ.

Does it not seem that the truth of all these shadows will be known through that revelation which occurs when, no longer "through a mirror and in an obscure manner" but "face to face," the holy ones will deserve to see the glory of God and to contemplate the causes and the truth of things? Because he had already, through the Holy Spirit, received an inkling of that truth, the apostle said, "Even if at one time we knew Christ according to the flesh, nevertheless we do not know him that way now" [2 Cor. 5:16].

These are the ideas that were able to make their way into our minds as we took up these very difficult questions about the incarnation and the deity of Christ. If someone comes up with better ideas and can confirm what he says with plainer assertions from the Holy Scriptures, let them be accepted instead of what we have written.

VI.

Athanasius

ORATIONS AGAINST THE ARIANS
Book III

(26) Just consider. Like people who do not grow weary in their impieties but are hardened in them after the fashion of Pharaoh, they hear and observe the Savior's human characteristics in the Gospel narratives but are perfectly forgetful, after the fashion of the Samosatene, of the Son's paternal divinity. With reckless boldness of speech they ask, "How can the Son be out of the nature of the Father and like the Father in essence when he says, 'All authority was given to me' [Matt. 28:18]; and 'The Father judges no one but has given all judgment to the Son' [John 5:22]; and 'The Father loves the Son and has put everything in his hand; the person who believes in the Son has eternal life' [John 3:35–36]; and again, 'Everything has been handed over to me by the Father, and no one knows the Father except the Son and anyone to whom the Son is willing to reveal him' [Matt. 11:27]; and again, 'Everything the Father gave me will come to me' [John 6:37]?" They then add, "If, as you assert, he was Son in virtue of his nature, he would have had no need to receive anything, but would have possessed it as Son in virtue of his nature.

"Moreover, how can he be, by nature and in truth, the power of the Father when he said, at the time of his suffering, 'Now my soul is troubled, and what shall I say? Father, save me from this hour. But this is the reason I have come to this hour. Father, glorify your name. There came, accordingly, a voice from heaven: "I have glorified it and I will glorify it again"' [John 12:27–28]. He says

83

the same sort of thing in another place: 'Father, if it be possible, let this cup pass from me' [Matt. 26:39]; and 'As Jesus was speaking, he was troubled in his spirit, and he bore witness and said, "Truly, truly I tell you, one of you will betray me"'" [John 13:21]. Furthermore, these malignant people argue, "If he had been power, he would not have been afraid, but rather would even have conveyed power to others."

Then they say, "If he was by nature the true and proper Wisdom of the Father, how does it stand written 'And Jesus grew in wisdom, in size, and in grace with God and with humans' [Luke 2:52]; or 'Coming into the region of Caesarea Philippi, he inquired of his disciples who people said him to be' [Matt. 16:13]? Also, when he came into Bethany, he inquired where Lazarus lay, and at a later time he said to his disciples, 'How many loaves do you have?' [Mark 6:38]. How, then," say they, "is this person Wisdom when he grows in wisdom and when he was ignorant of things which he expected to learn from others?"

Then, too, they have this question: "How can he be the proper Logos of the Father, without whom the Father has never existed, through whom, as you think, the Father made all things, when on the cross he said, 'My God, my God, why have you forsaken me?' [Matt. 27:46] and prior to this prayed, 'Glorify your name' [John 12:28] and 'Glorify me, Father, with the glory which you had with you before the cosmos existed' [John 17:5]? Also, he used to pray in desert places and would instruct his disciples to pray, lest they enter into temptation. Also he said, 'The spirit is eager but the flesh is weak' [Matt. 26:41]; and 'No one knows about that day or that hour, not the angels, and not the Son either'" [Mark 13:32].

Then, these wretched folk say, "If it were the case, as you conceive the matter, that the Son subsists eternally in the company of God, he would not have been ignorant of the day, but as Logos he would have known. And the one who subsists in the company of God would not have been forsaken, nor, since he already possessed it in the Father, would he have asked to receive glory, nor would he have prayed at all. Since he was the Logos, he would have needed nothing. Since, however, he is a human being, and one of the things which has come into existence, it is on that account that he spoke in this fashion and stood in need of what he did not possess. For it is characteristic of human beings to require and to need what they do not possess."

(27) This is the sort of thing these impious people say when they speak out.

If they argue in this way, however, they ought to carry their rashness a step further and ask, "Why did the Logos become flesh anyhow?" And to this query they might add, "How, being God, could he become a human being? How could something incorporeal be the bearer of a body?" Or they might, in the more Judaizing manner of Caiaphas, ask, "For what reason does Christ, being human, make himself God?" [cf. John 10:33].

These things, and others like them, are what the Jews used to mutter in the past as they gazed on Christ, and what the Ariomaniacs now disbelieve as they read about him and have fallen into blasphemy. If one sets the utterances of both groups alongside each other, one will certainly discover that they meet in a common disbelief, that they are equivalent in their rash impiety, and that they wage a common war against us.

The Jews used to say, "How, being human, can he be God?" while the Arians say, "If he was true God out of true God, how could he have become human?" Moreover, the Jews would take offense and speak mockingly—"He would not have suffered crucifixion if he had been the Son of God"—while the Arians, speaking from the other end of the spectrum, say to us, "How dare you assert that someone who has a body and so can suffer these things is the Logos who belongs to the essence of the Father?" Then, while the Jews sought to kill the Lord because "he claimed that God was his own Father, and made himself the equal of God" [John 5:18] as one who carried out the work which the Father does, the Arians have for their part learned to assert both that he is not the equal of God and that God is not by nature the proper Father of the Logos. Indeed, they seek to kill those who think these things. Again the Jews say, "Is not this the son of Joseph, whose father and mother we know? [John 6:42]. How then does he say, 'Before Abraham came to be, I am, and have come down out of heaven?'" [John 8:58]. And the Arians for their part reply to the same effect, "How can one who slept and cried and asked questions be Logos or God?" Both these groups deny the eternity and deity of the Logos on the ground of those human properties which he put up with on account of the flesh which was his own.

(28) Since this sort of madness is a Jewish thing, and Jewish in the way that Judas the traitor was Jewish, let them profess openly that they are disciples of Caiaphas and Herod and stop disguising Judaism with the name of Christianity. And let them, as we have said before, completely deny the appearance of the Savior in flesh (for this view harmonizes with their heresy). Or else, if they fear to be openly Jewish and to be circumcised because they do not want to displease Constantius and the people they have led astray, let them stop saying what the Jews said, for it is only fair to turn away from the opinions of those whose name they reject.

We are Christians, O you Arians, we are Christians! It is natural for us to have a close knowledge of the Gospels which concern the Savior—and neither to join the Jews in stoning him if we hear about his divinity and his eternity nor to join you in being offended at utterances of a lowly sort, which, as a human being, he voiced on our account. If you too want to become Christians, rid yourselves of Arius's madness and cleanse with the language of piety that hearing of yours which blasphemy has soiled. Know that when you cease being Arians you will also cease from the folly of the Jews, and that truth will immediately illumine you like light shining out of darkness.

Furthermore, you will no longer reproach us with saying that there are "two eternals." On the contrary, you will understand that the Lord is God's true and natural Son and that he is known to be not just eternal but one who exists concurrently with the eternity of the Father. There are things which are called "eternal" of which he is the Creator, for in Psalm 23 it is written, "Lift up your gates, O rulers, and be lifted up, O everlasting doors" [Ps. 24:7]. It is apparent, though, that these everlasting doors also came into being through his agency. But if he is himself the Creator of the things which are "everlasting," which of us can any longer doubt that he is more noble than these everlasting things and that he is made known as Lord not so much from his being eternal as from his being the Son of God? Being Son, he is inseparable from the Father, and there was not a "'when' when he did not exist." He always existed. Moreover, since he is the image and radiance of the Father, he also possesses the Father's eternity.

From our brief remarks it is possible to learn that the Arians stand convicted of misunderstanding the texts they brought forward as evidence. Furthermore, it is easy to see that they are revealed to have a flawed understanding by the texts from the Gospels which they are now bringing forward. The condition is that at this juncture we take hold of the basic meaning of the faith which belongs to us Christians, use it as a standard, and, as the apostle says, "apply ourselves to the reading of the inspired Scripture" [1 Tim. 4:13]. The enemies of Christ, being ignorant of the basic meaning of the faith, "have been led astray off the path of truth" [Wisd. of Sol. 5:6] and "have stumbled over the stone of stumbling" [Rom. 9:32], thinking "other than what they ought to think" [Rom. 12:3].

(29) What is the basic meaning and purport of Holy Scripture? It contains, as we have often said, a double account of the Savior. It says that he has always been God and is the Son, because he is the Logos and radiance and Wisdom of the Father. Furthermore, it says that in the end he became a human being, he took flesh for our sakes from the Virgin Mary, the God-bearer.

One can find this teaching indicated throughout Holy Scripture, as the Lord himself has said, "Search the Scriptures, for it is they which bear witness concerning me" [John 5:39]. Lest I write too much, however, by pulling together all the relevant texts, let me content myself with mention of John as representative. He says, "In the beginning was the Logos and the Logos was with God and the Logos was God. He was in the beginning with God. All things came to be through him, and apart from him not one thing came to be" [John 1:1–3]. He goes on, "And the Logos became flesh and dwelt among us, and we saw his glory—glory as of one uniquely born from the Father" [John 1:14]. Then there are Paul's words: "Who, being in the form of God, did not judge equality with God a thing to be clutched, but emptied himself, taking the form of a slave, coming to be in the likeness of human beings; and being found in the shape of a human being, he humbled himself and became obedient to the point of death, even death on a cross'' [Phil. 2:6–8].

Anyone who makes his way through the whole of Scripture with the meaning of these texts in mind will, on the basis of what they say, see how it is that the Father said to the Son in the beginning, "Let there be light" [Gen. 1:3] and "Let there be a firmament" [Gen. 1:6] and "Let us make humanity" [Gen. 1:26]. But at the consummation of the ages the Father sent the Son into the cosmos, "not in order to judge the cosmos, but in order that through him the cosmos might be saved" [John 3:17]. And it stands written: "Behold, a virgin shall conceive, and shall bear a son; and they shall call his name Emmanuel, which in translation means 'God with us'" [Matt. 1:23].

(30) So if someone wants to study Holy Scripture, let him learn from the ancient writers what it says, but from the Gospels let him perceive the Lord made a human being. For "the Word," John says, "was made flesh and dwelt among us" [John 1:14].

He became human. He did not enter into a human being. It is, moreover, crucial to recognize this. Otherwise, these impious people might fall into this error too and deceive some others, and these in their turn might suppose that just as in earlier times the Logos "came to be" in each of the saints, so even now he came into residence in a human being, sanctifying this one also and being revealed just as he was in the others. If this were the way of it, and all he did was to appear in a human being, there would have been nothing extraordinary, nor would those who saw him have been astonished and said, "Where does this man come from?" [Mark 4:41] and "Why do you, who are a human being, make yourself God?" [John 10:33], for since they heard the expression "and the word of the Lord came to" each of the prophets, they had some acquaintance with the idea.

Now, however, the Word of God, through whom everything came to be, has taken it on himself to become Son of man as well, and has "humbled himself, taking the form of a slave" [Phil. 2:7]. In consequence, the cross of Christ is "a scandal to the Jews," but to us Christ is "the power of God" and "the Wisdom of God"

[1 Cor. 1:23–24], for as John said, "the Word became flesh"—
Scripture being in the habit of calling the human being "flesh."
(As it says by Joel the prophet, "I will pour my spirit out on all
flesh" [Joel 2:28]. Similarly, Daniel said to Astyages: "I do not
worship idols made with hands, but the living God who created
the heaven and the earth and has dominion over all flesh" [Bel
and the Dragon 5]. For both he and Joel call humankind "flesh.")

(31) Therefore in former times he came to be with each of the
saints and sanctified those who truly received him. When they
were born, however, it was not said, "He has become a human
being"; nor, when they were suffering, was it said, "He has suffered." But when out of Mary he came amongst us "once for all at
the summing up of the ages for the putting away of sin" [Heb.
9:26]—for since he pleased to do so, the Father "sent his own Son,
born of a woman, born under the law" [Gal. 4:4]—on that occasion it is said that he took on flesh and became a human being and
suffered on our account in that flesh—even as Peter said, "Christ
therefore suffered on our account in the flesh" [1 Pet. 4:1]. The
purpose of this was to demonstrate and to bring all to believe that
although he is always God, and sanctifies those for whom he has
become present, and orders everything in accordance with the
Father's will, in the end and on our account he became a human
being, and "the Godhead dwelt bodily" [Col. 2:9], as the apostle
says, in the flesh. This amounts to saying, "Being God, he had his
own body, and using this as an instrument, he became a human
being on our account."

For this reason the things proper to this flesh are said to belong
to him because he was in it—such things as being hungry, being
thirsty, suffering, getting tired, and the like, to which the flesh is
susceptible. But the proper works of the Logos himself, such as
raising the dead and making the blind see and healing the woman
with a hemorrhage, he accomplished through the instrumentality
of his own body. Furthermore, the Logos bore the weaknesses of
the flesh as his own, since the flesh belonged to him, while the
flesh renders assistance in the works of the Godhead, since the
Godhead came to be within it, for it was God's body.

It is well that the prophet said "He *bore*" and did not say "He

89

cured our infirmities" [Matt. 8:17], lest, as one outside the body, he merely cured it as he has always done, and once again left human beings under the power of death. In fact, however, he bore our weaknesses and "he himself bore our sins" [Isa. 53:4], in order to show that he became a human being on our account and that the body which bore them in him is his very own. And he himself was in no way harmed as he "bore our sins in his body on the tree" [1 Pet. 2:24], to use Peter's words. We human beings, however, were set free from the passions which belonged to us and were filled with the righteousness of the Logos.

(32) Consequently, when the flesh was suffering, the Logos was not apart from it. That is why the suffering also is said to belong to him. When he was doing the works of the Father in a divine way, the flesh was not external to him. On the contrary, the Lord did these things in the body itself. This explains why, when he had become human, he said, "If I do not do the works of my Father, do not believe me. But if I do them, even if you do not believe me, believe the works themselves, so that you may know that the Father is in me and I in him" [John 10:37–38]. Thus, when it was necessary to raise up Peter's mother-in-law, who was suffering from a fever, it was a human act when he extended his hand but a divine act when he caused the disease to cease. Likewise, in the case of "the man blind from birth" [John 9:6] it was human spittle which he spat, but it was a divine act when he opened the man's eyes by means of clay. And where Lazarus is concerned, he uttered human speech in his capacity as a human being, but it was a divine act when, in his capacity as God, he raised Lazarus from the dead. It was in this fashion that these things were done, and they showed that he possessed a body in reality and not as a matter of mere seeming.

It was appropriate for the Lord, when he was clothed in human flesh, to put it on in its totality, together with all the passions proper to it, so that just as we say the body was properly his, so also the passions of the body might be said to belong to him alone, even though they did not touch him in his deity. So if the body had belonged to someone else, its passions too would be predicated of that subject. If, however, the flesh belongs to the Logos (for "the Logos became flesh"), it is necessary to predicate the fleshly passions of him whose flesh it is. And the one of whom the passions are predicated—condemnation, for example, scourging, and crucifixion and death and the other weaknesses of the body—is also the one to whom the triumph and the grace are attributed. So it is logical and fitting that passions of this sort be predicated not of another but of the Lord, in order that grace also may derive from him and we may become not worshipers of someone else but truly servants of God. We appeal not to something which has come into existence or to some ordinary human being but to the true Son who is by nature derived from God, and to this Son as he has become human and yet remains nothing other than our Lord and God and Savior.

(33) Who will not marvel at this? Who will not agree that it is truly something divine? If the works of the Logos' Godhead had not been done by means of the body, humanity would not have been divinized. Furthermore, if the properties of the flesh had not been reckoned to the Logos, humanity would not have been completely liberated from them. On the contrary, as I said above, they might have ceased for a brief space, but sin and corruption would have remained within humanity, just as they did in the case of human beings before Christ. What is more, this is apparent.

Many people, after all, have become holy and clean from all sin. Jeremiah was made holy even from the womb, and John, while still unborn, "leapt for joy" at the voice of Mary the mother of God. Nevertheless, "death reigned from Adam to Moses, even over those who had not sinned after the likeness of Adam's transgression" [Rom. 5:14], and in this way, human beings continued to be mortal and corruptible nonetheless, subject to the passions that belong to their nature.

Now that the Logos has become human and made the flesh his very own, these passions no longer affect the body because the Logos has come to dwell within it. In fact, the opposite is the case. The passions have been destroyed by him, and from now on human beings no longer continue as sinners and dead persons in accordance with the passions that are proper to them. Rather, they have risen from the dead in accordance with the power of the Logos, and they remain forever immortal and incorruptible.

This explains why he who supplies others with the origin of their being is himself said to have been born; his flesh was born of Mary the mother of God. The purpose of this is that we may have our origin relocated in him and that we may no longer return to earth because mere earth is what we are, but may be carried by him into the heavens because we are joined to the Logos who comes from heaven. In the same way, therefore, he has appropriately taken upon himself the other passions of the body too, in order that we may grasp eternal life no longer as human beings but as creatures belonging to the Logos, for we no longer die "in Adam" in accordance with our first origin. From now on, since our origin and all our fleshly weakness has been transferred to the Logos, we are being raised up from earth; the curse which sin occasioned has been removed through the agency of him who is in us and who "for our sakes became a curse" [Gal. 3:13]. Just as we die in Adam because we are all from the earth, so "we are all made alive in Christ" because we are "reborn" from above "by water and the Spirit" [1 Cor. 15:22; John 3:5]; the flesh is no longer earthly, but now it has been "logified" by the work of the divine Logos who on our account became flesh.

(34) In order that we may have a more exact understanding of the impassibility of the Logos' nature and of the weaknesses that are reckoned to him on account of his flesh, it is well to listen to the blessed Peter, for he will turn out to be a trustworthy witness where the Savior is concerned.

Peter writes in his letter, "Christ therefore suffered *in the flesh* for our sakes" [1 Pet. 4:1]. So when it is said that he hungered and thirsted and toiled and was ignorant and slept and cried out and made requests and fled and was born and turned away from the cup—in general, did all the things which belong to the flesh—let it in each case be said, as is fitting: "Christ hungered and thirsted 'for our sakes in the flesh'"; "Christ said he did not know and was beaten and toiled 'for our sakes in the flesh'"; and "Christ was lifted up and was born and grew up 'in the flesh'"; and "Christ was afraid and hid himself 'in the flesh' '"; and Christ said, 'If it is possible, let this cup pass from me,'" and "Christ was struck," and "Christ was receptive," "for our sakes in the flesh," In general, let all things of this sort be asserted as "for our sakes in the flesh," for this is precisely the reason the apostle himself said, "Christ therefore suffered" not in the Godhead but "for our sakes in the flesh," in order that the passions might be recognized to be natural properties not of the Logos but of the flesh.

So, then, let no one be scandalized by the human characteristics [of Christ]. Rather, let people see that the Logos himself is impassible by nature and that he nevertheless has these passions predicated of him in virtue of the flesh which he took on, since they are proper to the flesh and the body itself is proper to the Savior. Furthermore, he himself remains as he is—impassible in nature. He takes no hurt from these passions, but on the contrary destroys them and brings them to nothing. And human beings, because their own passions have been transferred to the impassible and abolished, are henceforth becoming impassible and free of them to all eternity. That is what John teaches when he says, "And know that he was manifested to take away our sins, and in him there is no sin" [1 John 3:5].

Since this is the case, no heretic will bring the following objection and ask, "What explains the fact that the flesh was raised when it is by nature mortal? And if it is raised, what explains the fact that it does not still hunger and thirst and suffer and remain mortal? For it came to be out of the earth, and how can it cease to be that which it is by nature?" Now the flesh can give an answer to the disputatious heretic: "I am indeed mortal by nature, taken from the earth. In the latter days, however, I have become the flesh of the Logos, and he himself has borne my passions, impassible though he is. So I am free of them. I am no longer enslaved to them, for the Lord has set me free from them. If you object because I have been released from the corruption which is mine by nature, see to it that you raise no objection to the fact that the divine Logos took to himself my state of slavery. Just as the Lord became a human being when he put on a body, so we human beings, once we have been connected to him by way of his flesh, are

93

divinized by the Logos, and from that point on we are the heirs of eternal life."

(35) We have necessarily begun by looking into these matters closely, so that if we see Christ acting or speaking in divine fashion through the instrumentality of his own body, we will know that he does these works because he is God; and again, so that if we see him speaking or suffering in the manner of a human being, we may not fail to understand that he became a human being by bearing flesh and that this is how he does and says these [human] things. If we recognize what is proper and peculiar to each, while at the same time perceiving and understanding that both sets of deeds come from one [agent], we believe rightly and shall never be led astray. But if anyone sees the things that are done divinely by the Logos and denies the body, or if anyone sees the things proper to the body and denies the enfleshed presence of the Logos or ascribes inferiority to the Logos because of his human character-istics—such a person, like a Jewish tavern-keeper who mixes water with the wine, will consider the cross a scandal or, like a Gentile, will judge the preaching to be foolishness. These are the sorts of things that have happened to God's enemies the Arians. They look at the human characteristics of the Savior and consider him to be a human being. So they ought also to look at the divine works of the Logos and deny the coming into existence of his body and rank themselves thenceforth with the Manichaeans. But, rather, let the latter finally learn that "the Logos became flesh," while we, who grasp the basic meaning and purport of the faith, know clearly that what they have misconstrued has a correct interpretation.

Consider these texts: "The Father loves the Son and has given everything into his hand" [John 3:35]; "Everything has been handed over to me by my Father" [Matt. 11:27]; "I can do no deed of myself, but I judge as I hear" [John 5:30]. As many such passages as there are, they do not demonstrate that there was a time when the Son did not possess these privileges. How can it be the case that the one who is the sole essential Logos and Wisdom of the Father should fail to possess eternally what the Father pos-sesses, especially when he also says, "Whatever things the Father possesses are mine" [John 16:15] and "The things which are mine belong to the Father" [John 17:10]? If the things which belong to the Father belong to the Son, while the Father possesses them eternally, it is plain that whatever the Son possesses, since it belongs to the Father, is in him eternally. Therefore, he did not make these statements because there was a time when these privileges were not his; he made them because even though the Son possesses eternally what he possesses, he nevertheless possesses them from the Father.

(36) There is a danger here. Someone who sees the Son in full possession of whatever belongs to the Father may, by reason of the unalterable similarity—not to say identity—of the qualities he possesses, blaspheme by being led astray after the fashion of Sabellius. Such a person may conclude that the Son is identical with the Father. It was for the sake of avoiding this error that he said "was given me" and "I received" and "was handed over to me," for the sole purpose of showing that he is not the Father but the Logos of the Father and the eternal Son, who on account of his likeness to the Father has *eternally* whatever he possesses from the Father, and on account of his being Son has *from the Father* whatever he possesses eternally. . . .

The expressions "was given" and "was handed over" do not imply that there was a time when [the Son] did not have these things. This—and the like conclusion where all such expressions are concerned—we can gather from a similar passage. The Savior himself says, "As the Father possesses life in himself, in the same manner also he has given the Son to have life in himself" [John 5:26]. By that phrase "he has given" he signifies that he is not himself the Father. When he says "in the same manner," he shows the Son's likeness of nature to the Father and the fact that he belongs to the Father. If there was a time when the Father did not possess life, obviously there was a time when the Son did not possess it either, for the Son possesses it "in the same manner" as the Father. If, however, it is irreligious to make this assertion, and, by contrast, is reverent to assert that the Father always possesses life, is it not absurd—when the Son states that he possesses life "in the same manner" as the Father—to assert that they possess it not "in the same manner" but differently? We conclude, rather, that the Logos is trustworthy and that everything he says he has received he possesses from the Father, though at the same time he possesses it eternally. Moreover, while the Father does not possess life from anyone, the Son possesses it from the Father.

It is like the case of radiance. Suppose that the radiance itself says, "The light has given me all places to illumine, and I illumine not from myself but as the light wills." In saying this, the radiance does not indicate that at one time it did not possess light but rather asserts, "I am proper to the light and everything which belongs to the light is mine." We ought to understand that this is so in the case of the Son, only more so, for when the Father has given everything to the Son, he still possesses everything in the Son, and when the Son possesses them, the Father still possesses them. The Son's deity is the deity of the Father, and in this way the Father carries out his providential care for all things in the Son.

(37) This is the way to understand sayings of that sort. But there is also a reverent understanding of the things that are said about the Savior in the fashion appropriate to a human being. That is why we examined statements of this sort earlier, so that if we hear him asking where Lazarus has been laid, or when, having come into the territory of Caesarea, he inquires, "Who do people say that I am?" [Matt. 16:13] or "How many loaves do you have?" [Mark 6:38] or "What do you want me to do for you?" [Matt. 20:32], we may see, on the basis of what we have already said, the right interpretation of these texts and not stumble as have those opponents of Christ, the Arians.

First we must ask the irreverent on what ground they judge that he is ignorant, for it is not always the case that a person who asks a question asks in ignorance. On the contrary, it is possible for one who has knowledge to ask about something he knows. John obviously knows that it is not ignorantly but with conscious knowledge that Christ asks, "How many loaves do you have?" for he writes, "This he said to test Philip; for he himself knew what he was going to do" [John 6:6]. But if he knew what he was doing, his question was not asked ignorantly but with knowledge.

Similar texts can be understood in the light of the treatment of this one. The Lord does not ask ignorantly when he inquires where

Lazarus has been laid or who people are saying that he is. Rather, he asks in knowledge of what he asks about, having grasped what he is going to do. And in this way their sophistry is briskly disposed of.

If they still want to argue because Christ asked questions, let them hear that there is no ignorance in the deity but that not knowing is, as has been said, proper to the flesh. The fact that this is so, moreover, can be seen from the fashion in which the Lord who inquired where Lazarus had been laid himself said—when he was not present, but a long way off—"Lazarus has died" [John 11:14], and where his death occurred. And this man whom they judge to be ignorant is the very one who knows the thoughts of his disciples ahead of time and knows what is in everyone's heart and "what is in the human person" [John 2:25]. What is more, he alone knows the Father and says, "I in the Father and the Father in me" [John 14:10].

(38) It is plain, therefore, to everyone that not knowing is proper to the flesh, whereas the Logos, insofar as he is the Logos, knows all things even before their origination. He has not ceased to be God by reason of becoming human, and he does not flee from things human because he is God. Far from it! On the contrary, it is as one who is God that he took on flesh, and it is as one who was in flesh that he divinized the flesh. Just as it was in the flesh that he asked questions, so it was in the flesh that he raised the dead man, and he demonstrated to all that one who gives life to the dead and calls the soul back is all the more one who knows the secrets of everything. Furthermore, he knew where Lazarus lay, yet he inquired about it. For the all-holy Logos of God, who endures everything for our sakes, did this also in order that just as he bore the burden of our ignorance so he might lavish [upon us] knowledge of his Father, the only true Father, and also knowledge of himself, who has been sent on our account to bring salvation to all. And there is no greater grace than that.

When, therefore (with regard to the texts they allege), the Savior says, "Authority was given me" and "Glorify your Son," and when Peter says, "Authority was given to him" we take all these passages in the same sense. All of them speak in a way appropriate to a human being because of [the Lord's] body. Even though he had need of nothing, he is nevertheless said to have been the recipient of the things he accepted in his capacity as a human being, in order that the grace he gives may be established through the fact that it is the Lord who has done the receiving and that the gift is lodged in him. A mere human being, though he does receive, also has the capacity to suffer deprivation. This fact was demonstrated in the case of Adam, who after receiving lost [what he had received]. But in order that grace may not be taken away, that it may be firmly guaranteed to people, he himself claims the gift as his own and says that, as a human being, he has received the authority which, as God, he possesses eternally. What is more, he who glorifies others says, "Glorify me," in order to show that his flesh has a need for these things. So it is that when his flesh has received this, he himself is said to have received, since that which receives it is in him and since he becomes a human being by receiving it.

(39) If, then, as we have said over and over, the Logos did not become a human being, then by all means let receiving and lacking glory and being ignorant characterize the Logos, as you say. But if he did become a human being (and he did), and it is a human being's part to receive and to stand in need and to be ignorant, why identify the giver as the receiver? Why suspect the one who supplies others of standing in need? Why set the Son apart from the Father by calling him imperfect and needy? Why deprive humanity of grace?

If the Logos himself, insofar as he is the Logos, receives and is glorified on his own account, and if, in his deity, he is the one who confers sanctification and the life of the resurrection, what sort of hope is there for the human race? Its members remain as they were —naked, unhappy, and dead—for they do not share in what is given to the Son. And why did the Logos dwell among us and become flesh? If the aim was that he should be the recipient of the benefits he is said to have received, it follows that he previously stood in need of these things; so he himself will be bound to give thanks to his body on the ground that when he entered the body he received from the Father these goods which had not belonged to him prior to his descent into the flesh. On the basis of this argument, it seems that he himself was bettered by means of the body rather than that the body was bettered through him. This, however, is a Jewish way of conceiving things.

If, on the other hand, the aim was for him to redeem the members of the human race, then the Logos did dwell among them, and in order to sanctify and divinize them, the Logos became flesh (for that is why he did it). To whom, then, is it not obvious that the things the Logos says he received when he became flesh are mentioned not on his own account but on account of the flesh? He spoke in the flesh, and the gifts bestowed by the Father through the Logos belonged to the flesh.

Let us see what he asked for and what he actually said he had received, so that in this way the latter can be understood. He asked for glory, then, and also said, "Everything has been handed over to me" [Matt. 11:27]. After his resurrection he says that he has received "all authority" [Matt. 28:18]. But even before he said "Everything has been handed over to me," he was the Lord of everything. "Everything came to be through him" [John 1:3] and there was "one Lord, through whom are all things" [1 Cor. 8:6]. And he who asks for glory was and is "the Lord of glory," as Paul says: "For if they had known, they would not have crucified the Lord of glory" [1 Cor. 2:8]. He possessed what he asked for when he said, ". . . with the glory which I possessed in your presence before the world existed."

(40) Furthermore, the authority he said he received after the resurrection is an authority he possessed both before he received it and before the resurrection. He himself in his own right rebuked Satan, saying, "Get behind me, Satan" [Matt. 4:10], and he "gave" the disciples "authority" over Satan when he also said, on their return to him, "I saw Satan like a star fallen from heaven" [Luke 10:18].

But again, he is shown to be in possession of that which he says he has received even before he received it, for he cast out the demons and set loose what Satan had bound (as he did in the case of Abraham's daughter), and he remitted sins, saying to the paralytic and to the woman who anointed his feet, "Your sins are forgiven you" [Matt. 9:5; Luke 7:48]. He also raised the dead and restored the original state of the blind man by granting him sight. What is more, he did these things not as one who was coming to the time when he would receive authority but as one "full of authority" [Isa. 9:6 LXX].

On the basis of all this, it is obvious that what he possessed as Logos he claimed to have received in his capacity as a human being, both after his becoming a human being and after his resurrection. The purpose and point of this is that from now on, through his mediation, human beings, made "sharers in the divine nature" (2 Pet. 1:4), have authority over demons on the earth, while in the heavens, "being set free from corruption" [Rom. 8:21], they will reign eternally. It is necessary in general to recognize that he did not receive any of the things he says he received without already possessing them, for the Logos possessed them eternally as God. It is in virtue of his being human that we now say "he received," with a view to asserting that since the flesh was, in him, the recipient, from now on the gift it received stands as a sure reality which comes from that flesh to us. Peter's words—"He received honor and glory from God, with the angels being subjected to him" [2 Pet. 1:17; 1 Pet. 3:22]—also have the same general sense. Just as he asked questions in his capacity as a human being and raised Lazarus in his capacity as God, so the words "he received" are said of him in his human reality, while the subjection of the angels gives evidence of the deity of the Logos.

(41) So give over, then, you despisers of God, and do not humiliate the Logos! Nor, on the ground of needfulness or ignorance, deprive him of his deity, which is the Father's own, lest you belabor the Christ with your allegations in the same way as did the Jews who used in those days to stone him. These things of which we have been speaking do not belong to the Logos insofar as he is Logos; they belong, rather, to human beings. Moreover, we do not label as human the great deeds he did when he spat and stretched out his hand and summoned Lazarus. Even though they were accomplished through the body, we call them God's deeds. On the same principle, if human characteristics are attributed to the Savior in the gospel, we take account, in this case too, of the nature of

what is being said. And since it is foreign to God, we do not reckon it to the deity of the Logos but to his humanity, for even though "the Logos became flesh," the passions are nevertheless proper to the flesh, and even though the flesh became, in the Logos, a bearer of the divine, nevertheless the grace and power come from the Logos. To be sure, he does the works of the Father through the medium of the flesh, but the passions of the flesh are no less evident in him. I mean that he asked questions and raised Lazarus, and he rebuked his mother by saying, "My hour is not yet come" —and immediately he made the water wine. He was true God in the flesh, and he was true flesh in the Logos. That is why, by his works, he revealed both the fact that he is God's Son and his own Father and, by the passions of his flesh, that he bore a real body and that this body was his very own.

VII.

Apollinaris of Laodicea

ON THE UNION IN CHRIST OF THE BODY
WITH THE GODHEAD

(1) Rightly is the Lord confessed to have been a child who was holy from the beginning, even in what concerns his body. And in this regard he differs from every other body, for he was conceived in his mother not in separation from the Godhead but in union with it, just as the angel says, "The holy Spirit shall come upon you, and the power of the Most High shall overshadow you, so that your holy offspring will be called Son of God" [Luke 1:35]. Moreover, there was a heavenly descent, not merely a birth from a woman; it is said not only "Born of a woman, born under the Law" [Gal. 4:4] but also "No one shall ascend into heaven, save he who came down from heaven, the Son of man" [John 3:13]. (2) And it is not possible to take the body separately and call it a creature, since it is altogether inseparable from him whose body it is. Rather, it shares in the title of the uncreated and in the name of God, because it is conjoined into unity with God, just as it is said that "the Word became flesh" [John 1:14] and, by the apostle, "The last Adam became a life-giving Spirit" [1 Cor. 15:45].

(3) Just as we attribute glory to the body by reason of the divine conjunction and its unity with God, so we ought not to deny the inglorious attributes that stem from the body. These are, in the words of the apostle, "to be born of a woman" [Gal. 4:4] and, in the words of the prophet, "to have been formed from the womb as a slave to God" [Isa. 49:5], really to be named "human being" and "Son of man" and to be reckoned later than Abraham by the

103

many generations after which he became man. (4) Indeed, it is necessary to speak and to hear [of him] in human terms, even as, when he is called truly a human being, no one will deny the divine essence which, together with the body, that title signifies; and when he is called a slave by reason of his body, no one will deny the royal nature which, together with the body, is signified by name of slavery; and again, when a heavenly man is said to have descended from heaven, no one will deny that the earthly body is knit together with the Godhead. He is not divided either in fact or in name when, by reason of his conjunction with the form of a slave and with the created body, the Lord is called a slave, and the uncreated is styled "made."

(5) The confession is that in him the creature is in unity with the uncreated, while the uncreated is commingled with the creature, so that one nature is constituted out of the parts severally, and the Word contributes a special energy to the whole together with the divine perfection. The same thing happens in the case of the ordinary man, made up as he is of two incomplete parts which together fill out one nature and are signified by one name; for at the same time the whole is called "flesh" without the soul's being thereby stripped away, and the whole is styled "soul" without the body's being stripped away (if, indeed, it is something else alongside the soul). (6) So the God who became human, the Lord and ruler of all that comes to be, may have come to be of a woman, yet he is Lord. He may have been formed after the fashion of slaves, yet he is Spirit. He may be proclaimed as flesh because of his union with the flesh, yet according to the apostle he is not a human being; and though he is preached as human by the same apostle, yet he calls the whole Christ invisible God transformed by a visible body, uncreated God made manifest in a created garment. He emptied himself after the fashion of a slave, but in his divine essence he is unemptied and unaltered and undiminished (for no alteration can affect the divine nature), neither is he decreased or increased.

(7) When he says, "Glorify me," this utterance stems from the body, and the glorification touches the body, but the reference is to Christ as a whole, because the whole is one. He adds, ". . . with the glory which I possessed with you before the existence of the world" [John 17:5] and manifests the eternally glorious Godhead,

but though this expression peculiarly befits the Godhead, it was spoken inclusively with reference to the whole. (8) Thus he is both coessential with God in the invisible Spirit (the flesh being comprehended in the title because it has been united to that which is coessential with God), and again coessential with men (the Godhead being comprehended with the body because it has been united to what is coessential with us). And the nature of the flesh is not altered by its union with what is coessential with God and by its participation in the title of *homoousios*, even as the nature of the Godhead is not changed by its participation of a human body and by bearing the name of a flesh coessential with us.

(9) When Paul said, ". . . who was begotten of the seed of David according to the flesh" [Rom. 1:3], he meant that the Son of God was so born, and he did not name the flesh as something separate and say, "The flesh was born of the seed of David." When he says, "Let this mind be in you which was also in Christ Jesus, who being in the form of God, did not judge equality with God a thing to be grasped at" [Phil. 2:5-6], he did not make a division and say, "Whose Godhead, [being] in the form of God the Logos, did not judge equality with God a thing to be snatched at." And yet the Godhead was not named "Jesus" before his birth from a virgin; neither did it receive the chrism of the holy Spirit, because the Word of God is the giver of the Spirit, not the one who is sanctified by the Spirit.

(10) Furthermore, he says, "On their account I sanctify myself, in order that they themselves may be sanctified in truth" [John 17:19]. He does not make a division and say, "I sanctify the flesh." Rather, he makes a conjunction and says, "I sanctify myself," even though, for anyone who considers the matter with care, it is not possible for him to be the agent of his own sanctification, for if the whole sanctifies, what is sanctified? And if the whole is sanctified, what is the sanctifying agent? Nevertheless, he preserves the one person and the indivisible manifestation of one life, and attributes both the act of sanctifying and the sanctification which results to the whole Christ. This he does in order that it may be clear and certain to us that one agent does not sanctify another in the prophetic or apostolic fashion—as the Spirit sanctifies the prophets and apostles (just as Paul says, concerning the

whole church, "called to be saints and sanctified in Christ Jesus" [1 Cor. 1:2], and the Savior himself says concerning the apostles, "Sanctify them in truth" [John 17:17]. (11) For humankind as a whole is involved in being sanctified, not in sanctifying. And the angelic order, like the whole creation, is being sanctified and illuminated, while the Spirit sanctifies and illuminates. But the Logos sanctifies and illuminates through the Spirit, being in no wise sanctified, for the Logos is Creator and not creature. Here, however, there is sanctification, and embodiment as well, and though the two things are distinct, they are one by reason of the union of the flesh with the Godhead, so that there is no separation of one which sanctifies and another which is sanctified, and the incarnation itself is in every way a sanctification.

(12) To those who said, "You, being a man, make yourself God" [John 10:33], the Savior gave, by way of reply, the rationale of his own manhood. He said, "Do you say, 'You blaspheme,' to him whom the Father sanctified and sent into the world, because I said, 'I am the Son of God'?" [John 10:36]. What sanctification is this of which he speaks, save the sanctification of the flesh by the Godhead? For in these circumstances the body lives by the sanctification of the Godhead and not by the provision of a human soul, and the whole is completely joined in one. Moreover, his saying "whom the Father sanctified and sent" means that the sanctifier is sanctified together with that which is sanctified; he attaches the sanctifier to that which is sanctified. (13) Elsewhere he explains this sanctification [by saying] that it was the birth from a virgin. "For to this end was I born and to this end did I come into the world, that I might bear witness to the truth" [John 18:37]. The ordinary man is ensouled and lives by the will of the flesh and the will of the husband; the spermatic substance which is emitted carries the life-giving power into the receptive womb. But the holy child born of the Virgin was constituted by the coming of Spirit and the overshadowing of power. A spermatic substance did not bring about the divine life; rather, a spiritual and divine power afforded a divine conception to the Virgin and gave the gift of the divine offspring.

(14) Thus, both the exaltation of Christ and his being accorded the name above every name [took place] in accordance with the

manner of the union, even though the exaltation is proper to the flesh which ascended from below. But because the flesh does not ascend by itself, the whole [Christ] is inclusively termed "exalted," and the reception of grace is connected with him in virtue of the flesh which was brought from humiliation to glory, for grace does not add glory to the ever-glorious Word; what was existing and abiding existed in the form of God and was equal to God.

(15) Even in the flesh the Lord says that he is equal to God, since according to John he says that God is his own Father and he makes himself equal to God. What he possesses he cannot receive, even as, because the flesh receives what it does not possess (impassibility instead of affliction with passions, a heavenly instead of an earthly way of life, royal authority instead of slavery in subjection to men, being worshiped by the whole creation instead of giving worship to another), his being graced with the name above every name is ascribed to the whole [Christ]. (16) Furthermore, if anyone dares to separate mention of grace from the Name above every name, neither of the two will be properly spoken, for if the gift is to the Word as to one who does not possess it, the Name above every name is no longer given by grace. And if he possesses this not by gift but by nature (as he does possess it in his Godhead), then it is not possible that this be given him. (17) Of necessity, therefore, both that which is corporeal and that which is divine are predicated of the whole Christ. And the man who cannot, in different things which are united, recognize what is characteristic of each shall fall clumsily into contradictions, but he who both acknowledges the distinctive characteristics and preserves the union shall neither falsify the nature nor be ignorant of the union.

FRAGMENTS

9. If the same one is a complete human being and God as well, and the pious spirit does not worship a human being but worships God, it will be found both worshiping and not worshiping the same person—which is impossible. Moreover, humanity itself does not judge itself to be an object of worship . . . but God knows himself to be an object of worship. Yet it is inconceivable that the

107

same person should both know himself to be an object of worship and not know it. Therefore, it is inconceivable that the same person should be both God and an entire man. Rather, he exists in the singleness of an incarnate divine nature which is commingled [with flesh], with the result that worshipers bend their attention to God inseparable from his flesh and not to one who is worshiped and one who is not. . . .

10. O new creation and divine mixture! God and flesh completed one and the same nature!

17. The human being who is come down from heaven is not, he says, a human being from earth; yet, though he came down from heaven, he is a human being, for in the Gospels the Lord does not repudiate this title.

18. But if the Son of man is from heaven and the Son of God is born of woman, how is it not the case that the same one is God and a human being?

19. But (he says) he is God in virtue of the Spirit which is enfleshed but human in virtue of the flesh assumed by God.

22. But the flesh is not soulless, for it is said to fight against the spirit and to resist the law of the intellect, and we say that even the bodies of beasts without reason are endowed with soul.

25. So Christ, having God as his spirit—that is, his intellect—together with soul and body, is rightly called "the human being from heaven."

26. And Paul calls the first Adam a soul together with a body.

28. Wherefore Paul calls the first Adam a soul which is together with a body and not without a body, but which gives its name to the whole man, even though of itself the soul is called soul in such a way as to include spirit.

38. By this it is transparently clear that the very human being who speaks to us the things of the Father is God the Creator of the ages, "the radiance of his glory, the impress of his substance," inasmuch as he is God in his own spirit and not another besides God who has God inside him. He himself, by his own agency, that is to say, through his flesh, purified the world of sin.

41. By this means the prophetic word reveals that he is coessential with God not according to the flesh but according to the Spirit which is united with the flesh.

42. Behold the preexisting equality of the same Jesus Christ with his Father, his subsequently acquired likeness to human beings. And what more surely than this shows that he is not one together with another, complete God together with complete man?

45. He is not a human being but is like a human being, since he is not coessential with humanity in his highest part.

69. For he would not have been born in the likeness of a human being unless, like a human being, he was in fact an incarnate intellect.

70. If the Lord is not incarnate intellect, he must be Wisdom enlightening the intellect of a human being. But this happens in the case of all human persons, and if this is the way of it, then the coming of Christ is not a visit from God but the birth of a human being.

71. If the Word did not become intellect incarnate but was Wisdom within the intellect, the Lord did not come down or empty himself.

72. And in this way he was human, for a human being, according to Paul, is an intellect in the flesh.

74. If together with God, who is intellect, there was also a human intellect in Christ, then the work of the incarnation is not accomplished in him. But if the work of the incarnation is not accomplished in the self-moved and undetermined intellect, then this work, which is the destruction of sin, is accomplished in the flesh, which is moved from without and energized by the divine Intellect. The self-moved intellect within us shares in the destruction of sin insofar as it assimilates itself to Christ.

76. Therefore, the human race is saved not by the assumption of an intellect and of a whole human being but by the assumption of flesh, whose nature it is to be ruled. What was needed was unchangeable Intellect which did not fall under the domination of the flesh on account of its weakness of understanding but which adapted the flesh to itself without force.

85. The Lord's flesh is worshiped, inasmuch as together with him it is one person and one living organism.

87. If anyone thinks that one human being was united to God beyond all men and angels, he will deprive men and angels of self-determination, just as the flesh is without self-determination. But

to be deprived of self-determination is the destruction of a self-determining creature, and no nature is destroyed by him who made it. Therefore a human being was not united to God.

89. If, then, a human being is made up of three parts, the Lord is also a human being, for the Lord surely is made up of three parts: spirit and soul and body. But he is the heavenly human being and life-giving Spirit.

91. On the other hand, if we are made up of three parts, while he is made up of four, he is not a human being but a man-God.

93. He cannot save the world while remaining a human being and being subject to the common destruction of humans, but neither are we saved by God, except as he is mingled with us. In becoming flesh (that is, human), however, he is mingled with us, just as the gospel says, when he became flesh, then he tabernacled among us. But neither does he loose the sin of men unless he became a man unable to sin, and neither does he destroy the rule of death that oppresses all men, unless he died and rose as a man.

108. Christ is one, moved only by a divine will, just as we know that his activity is one, manifested in different marvels and sufferings of his one nature, for he is believed to be God enfleshed.

109. The saying "Father, if it is possible let this cup pass from me; nevertheless not mine but your will be done" [Matt. 26:39] signifies not that there are the wills of two different subjects who do not agree with each other but rather that there is the will of one and the same subject, divinely activated, but for the sake of the incarnation asking to be spared death, because the one who speaks these words is flesh-bearing God, and there is no division within his will.

117. God who has taken to himself an instrument of activity is both God insofar as he activates and human with respect to the instrument of activity which he uses. Remaining God, he is not altered. The instrument and its user naturally produce a single action, but if the action is one, the essence (*ousia*) is one also. Therefore, there has come to be one essence of the Logos and his instrumental means of activity.

123. That which is simple is one, but that which is made up of parts cannot be one, so the person who says that the Word became

flesh predicates change of the one Word. But if, as in the case of a human being, that which is made up of parts is also one, then the person who, on account of the union with the flesh, says "the Word became flesh" asserts that the Word is one in the fashion of something made up of parts.

124. Incarnation means emptying, but the emptying did not reveal a man. Rather, it revealed the Son of man who "emptied himself" not by being changed but by being clothed.

126. In their irrational body, people are coessential with irrational animals, but insofar as they are rational (*logikoi*), they are of a different essence. So also God, who is coessential with men in his flesh, is of a different essence insofar as he is Logos and God.

127. The qualities of things which are mixed together are mixed and not destroyed, so that certain portions stand apart from the elements that have been mixed, as wine does from water. There is neither a mingling with body nor a mingling of the sort which occurs between bodies, which does not preserve an unmixed element, with the result that, as it is needful from time to time, the activity of the Godhead either withdraws or is mingled—as it occurred in the case of the Lord's fasting. When the Godhead, in its superiority to need, was mingled [with the body], hunger was forestalled. But when [divine] superiority to need was not opposed to craving, hunger came upon him—to the devil's destruction. If the mingling of bodies knew no change, however, how much more that of the Godhead?

128. If the mixture with iron, which shows the iron itself to be fire insomuch as it does the work of fire, does not change its nature, neither does the union of God with the body involve an alteration of the body, even though the body may extend its divine energies to those things that can be touched by it.

129. If a human being has both a soul and a body, and these remain themselves when they are in unity, how much more does Christ, having Godhead and body, retain both conserved and not confused?

VIII.

Theodore of Mopsuestia

FRAGMENTS OF THE DOCTRINAL WORKS
On the Incarnation, Book V   Fragment 1

Whenever anyone distinguishes the natures [of Christ], he must necessarily discover first one and then another. I doubt that even [my opponents] will deny this fact, since it is granted that by nature God the Logos is one thing and that which was assumed (whatever it may be) is another. Nevertheless, [Christ] is likewise discovered to be the same in person—by no means as the result of a confusion of natures but by reason of the union which came about of the one assumed to the One who assumes him. For if it is rightly granted that the former is different from the latter in nature, it is also obvious that the one assumed is not equal to the One who assumes him. Plainly he will be found to be one and the same by a union in the order of person.

It is obligatory, therefore, to make a distinction in this way among the attributes of Christ, for there is nothing to oppose such a distinction. In fact, it is in close accord with the Scriptures. When matters are understood this way, there arises neither a confusion of the natures nor any perverse division of the person. Let the character of the natures stand without confusion, and let the person be acknowledged as undivided—the former in virtue of the characteristic property of the nature, since the one assumed is distinct from the One who assumes him, and the latter in virtue of the personal union, since the One who assumes and the nature of the one assumed are included in the denotation of a single name. Then, if I may phrase it so, in using the word "son," we are at one and the

113

same time calling upon God the Word and signifying the assumed nature because of the union it has with him.

On the Incarnation, Book VII   Fragment 2

If we learn how the indwelling takes place, we shall know both the general mode of the indwelling and its differentiating mark. To get on, then, some assert that the indwelling took place by *essence,* and others that it took place by *active operation.* So let us ask whether either of these assertions is correct.

First, let us be told whether [God] dwells in everyone or not. It is evident that God's indwelling is not in everyone, for God promises such indwelling to the saints as something exceptional, or, speaking generally, to those whom he wishes to be dedicated to him—or else why did he once promise, "I will dwell among them and walk among them, and I will be their God and they shall be my people" [Lev. 26:12], as though he were bestowing on them something out of the ordinary, if in fact all people shared in this? Hence, if he does not dwell in all (which is evident)—I do not mean "in all beings" but "in all humans"—there must of necessity be some special kind of indwelling according to which he is present only in those in whom he is specifically said to dwell.

It is, then, most inappropriate to say that God indwells by his *essence,* for in that case, either his essence must be limited exclusively to those in whom he is said to dwell, and he will be external to all others (which is an impossible conclusion because of God's boundless nature, which is present everywhere and circumscribed by no spatial boundaries), or else, if it be asserted that God is present everywhere in virtue of his essence, then absolutely all things must share in his indwelling—no longer only humans but also irrational animals and even lifeless things, if we say that the indwelling is effected in them by essence. Now both these conclusions are evidently unseemly, for to say that God dwells in all things is downright absurd, and to circumscribe his essence is out of the question. Therefore, to say that the indwelling takes place by essence would be quite simpleminded.

The same thing might be said in the case of *active operation,* for it is necessary in this case too for God to limit his operation to those in whom he dwells. How, then, will our word be true—that God foreknows everything and governs all things and actively works in all things what is suitable? Contrariwise, suppose that everything shares in his active operation. This is indeed fitting and logical, since all things are empowered by him, in that he both constitutes every creature in existence and enables it to operate according to its own nature. We should then say that he dwells in everything. Therefore, it is impossible to say that God makes his indwelling either by his essence or, further, by his active operation.

What is left, then? What explanation shall we use which, when we maintain it, will in these matters be manifestly appropriate?

It seems evident, we shall say, that the indwelling should fittingly be described as taking place by *good pleasure*. And *good pleasure* means that best and noblest will of God, which he exercises when he is pleased with those who are zealous to be dedicated to him, because of their excellent standing in his sight. This is the customary usage of Scripture and is assumed there. Thus the blessed David writes, "He does not delight in the strength of the horse; he takes no pleasure in the legs of a man. The Lord takes pleasure in those who fear him, in those who hope in his mercy" [Ps. 146:10–11 LXX]. He says this because God does not see fit to assist others, nor does he wish to work together with any but those who, it says, "fear him." Of these he makes great account, and he sees fit to work together with them and to come to their aid.

It is, therefore, proper to speak of the indwelling in this fashion, for since God exists boundless and uncircumscribed by nature, he is present with all. But by "good pleasure" he is far from some and near to others; for Scripture says, following this conception, "The Lord is nigh unto them that are of a broken heart; and he saves such as are of a contrite spirit" [Ps. 33:19 LXX]. Elsewhere it says, "Cast me not away from thy presence, and take not the holy Spirit from me" [Ps. 1:13 LXX]. By inclination he is present to those who are worthy of such nearness, but he is far from sinners. It is not by nature, however, that he is either separated from some or closer to others; he effects both relationships by the disposition of his will.

This is the way in which he is near and far by virtue of his good pleasure (for it is quite clear from what we have previously said what we mean by "good pleasure"; it was to make this clear that we took such great pains to establish the meaning of the word). And in the same way, by his good pleasure, he perfects his indwelling, not confining his essence or his active operation to those whom he indwells and remaining apart from the rest, but remaining present to all by his essence and separate from those who are unworthy by the disposition of his grace. In this way his limitlessness is the better preserved to him, since it is not made to seem that his very limitlessness subjects him to an external necessity. For if he were present everywhere by good pleasure, he would be seen to be subjected in another way to external necessity, since he would effect his presence no longer by will but by the boundlessness of his nature, and his will would be subservient to that. But since he is present to all by nature and is separated from whom he wishes by will, no one who is unworthy is profited by God's presence, while the true and pure limitlessness of his nature is preserved to him.

In this way, therefore, he is present to some by good pleasure and separated from others—present with these just as if he were separated from the others by essence. Just as the indwelling takes place by good pleasure, so also his good pleasure alters the mode of his indwelling. That which effects the indwelling of God, and makes him known as present everywhere by his essence while he indwells (by good pleasure, I mean) a very few, also altogether determines the mode of his indwelling. Just as he is present to all by essence, but is said to dwell not in all but only in those to whom he is present by good pleasure, so too, even though he be said to indwell, yet his indwelling is not all of a kind; even the mode of indwelling will vary in proportion to his good pleasure.

Therefore, whenever he is said to indwell either the apostles or just persons generally, he makes his indwelling as one who takes pleasure in those who are righteous, as one who takes delight in people who are duly virtuous. But we do not say that God's indwelling took place in Christ in this way, for we could never be so insane as that. On the contrary, the indwelling took place in him *as in a son*; it was in this sense that he took pleasure in him and indwelt him.

But what does it mean to say "as in a son"? It means that having indwelt him, he united the one assumed as a whole to himself and equipped him to share with himself in all the honor in which he, being Son by nature, participates, so as to be counted one person in virtue of the union with him and to share with him all his dominion, and in this way to accomplish everything in him, so that even the examination and judgment of the world shall be fulfilled through him and his advent. Of course, in all this the difference in natural characteristics is kept in mind.

On the Incarnation, Book VII   Fragment 3

Therefore, just as we, if we come at last to the future state, shall be perfectly governed by the Spirit in body and soul but now possess a kind of partial firstfruits of that condition inasmuch as, being aided by the Spirit, we are not compelled to heed the counsels of the soul, so also the Lord, although at a later stage he had the Logos of God working within him and throughout him in a perfect way, so as to be inseparable from the Logos in his every motion, even before this had as much as was needed for accomplishing in himself the mighty things required. Before his crucifixion, because it was needful, he was permitted to fulfill by his own purposes a righteousness which was for our sake, and even in this undertaking he was urged on by the Logos and strengthened for the perfect fulfillment of what was fitting, for he had union with the Logos straightway from the beginning when he was formed in his mother's womb. And when he arrived at maturity, when there comes to natural birth in human persons a judgment as to what is good and what is not (rather, even before this age), he demonstrated a much quicker and more acute power of judgment in this regard than others. Indeed, even among ordinary human beings the power of judgment is not born in all alike at the same time; some pursue what is needful more quickly and with greater purpose, and others acquire this skill only in greater time by training. This quality in him—which was exceptional by comparison to others—came to birth in him sooner than the usual age in others. And it was suitable that he should have something beyond the ordinary in his human qualities, because he was not born according to the common nature of human beings, of a man and a woman, but was fashioned by the divine energy of the Spirit.

He had an inclination beyond the ordinary toward nobler things because of his union with God the Logos, of which also he was deemed worthy by the foreknowledge of God the Logos, who united him to himself from above. So for all these reasons he was immediately possessed, together with judgment, of a great hatred for evil, and with indissoluble love he molded himself to the good, receiving also the cooperation of God the Logos in proportion to his own purpose. From that point he was preserved, unchangeable, from alteration for the worse. On the one hand, he held fast to this way by his own will, while on the other hand this purpose was faithfully guarded in him by the cooperating work of God the Logos. And he progressed with the greatest ease toward a consummate virtue, whether in keeping the Law before his baptism or in following the citizenship in grace after his baptism. He furnishes us a type of this citizenship and is himself a way, so to speak, established for this end. Thus, later, after the resurrection and ascension, when he had shown himself worthy of the union by his own will (having received the union even before this in his very fashioning, by the good pleasure of the Lord), he also unmistakably furnished for ever after the proof of the union, since he had nothing to separate and cut him off from the working of God the Logos but had God the Logos accomplishing everything in him through the union.

On the Incarnation, Book VII   Fragment 4

The unity of person is recognized by the fact that (the Word) accomplishes everything through him. This unity is effected by the indwelling according to good pleasure. For this reason, in asserting that the Son of God will come as judge from heaven, we understand at one and the same time the advent both of the man and of

God the Word, not because God the Word is degraded to be similar to him in nature, but because by good pleasure there will be a unity with him wherever he is, since through him the Logos accomplishes everything.

On the Incarnation, Book VII   Fragment 5

"And Jesus increased in age and in wisdom and in grace with God and humans" [Luke 2:52]. He increased in age, to be sure, because time moved on, and in wisdom because he acquired understanding to match his advancing years. But he increased in grace by pursuing the virtue which is attendant upon understanding and knowledge. Because of this, the grace which was his from God received assistance, and in all these ways he advanced in the sight of God and men. People observed this growth, and God not only observed it but also testified to it and bestowed his cooperation in what was happening. Therefore, it is plain that he fulfilled virtue more exactly and more easily than was possible for other people, since God the Logos, with his foreknowledge of the sort of person one will turn out to be, had united Jesus with himself in his very conception and furnished him with a fuller cooperation for the accomplishment of what was necessary. The Logos governed everything which concerned him for the sake of the salvation of all humankind, and he urged him on toward a larger perfection, the while lightening for him the greater part of his toils, whether they were of the soul or of the body. In this way he prepared him for a more perfect and an easier fulfillment of virtue.

On the Incarnation, Book VII   Fragment 6

The one who was assumed according to foreknowledge was united with God from the very beginning, since he received the foundation of the union in his very fashioning in his mother's womb. And since he had already been found worthy of the union, he obtained all that could properly be obtained by a man united to the Only Begotten and Ruler of the universe, and he was counted worthy of higher gifts than the rest of humanity as the special endowment of the union came to be his. Thus he was the first to be

119

found worthy of the indwelling of the Spirit in a degree surpassing the rest of humanity—and worthy of it in a different way from the rest of humanity. He received the whole grace of the Spirit within himself and furnished to others a partial participation in the whole Spirit. So, too, it came about that the Spirit in its wholeness worked within him. What was spoken, so far as the utterance of the sound went, was human, but the power of what was said was something different and mighty.

On the Incarnation, Book VIII　　　　　　　　　Fragment 7

In every way, then, it is clear in the first place that the notion of "mixture" is both exceptionally unsuitable and incongruous, since each of the natures remains indissolubly in itself. Moreover, it is also quite evident that the notion of "union" is thoroughly congruous, for by means of it the natures which are brought together make up one person according to the union. Thus, when the Lord says of man and woman, "Wherefore they are no longer two, but one flesh" [Matt. 19:6], we may say, in accordance with the logic of union, 'They are no longer two persons but one," even though, obviously, the natures are distinct. Just as in the example of marriage the mention of unity of flesh is not contradicted by the duality of subjects, so in the case of Christ the personal union is not destroyed by the distinction of natures. When we distinguish the natures, we speak of the nature of God the Word as complete and of his person as complete (for there is no hypostasis without its person). Moreover, the nature of the man is complete, and likewise his person. But when we consider the union, then we speak of one person.

On the Incarnation, Book VIII　　　　　　　　　Fragment 8

In the same way we say that the essence of God the Word is his own and that the essence of the man is *his* own, for the natures are distinct, but the person effected by the union is one. In this way, when we try to distinguish the natures, we say that the person of the man is complete and that that of the Godhead is complete. But when we consider the union, then we proclaim that both natures are one person, since the humanity receives from the divinity honor surpassing that which belongs to a creature, and the divinity brings to perfection in the man everything that is fitting

On the Incarnation, Book IX   Fragment 9

In any case, if the expression "the Logos became flesh" refers to a process of alteration, what is to be understood by "he dwelt"? It is plain to everyone that what indwells is different from what is indwelt. . . . For "he dwelt among us," assuming and indwelling our nature, and working in it everything pertaining to our salvation. How, then, did God the Word *become* flesh by indwelling? Obviously not because he was changed or altered; otherwise there would have been no mention of indwelling.

On the Incarnation, Book IX   Fragment 10

For what in our case is spoken of according to its disposition in space is spoken of in the case of God according to the disposition of his will. As we say of ourselves, "I was in this place," so also we say of God that he was in this place, since what movement brings about in our case is effected by will in the case of God, because by nature he is present everywhere.

On the Incarnation, Book XII   Fragment 11

Let no one be deceived by the artfulness of their questions. It is disgraceful (as the apostle says) to set aside so great a cloud of witnesses and, deceived by clever questions, to be joined with the party of our opponents. What is it that they artfully ask? "Is Mary a man's mother or God's mother?" And then, "Who was crucified, God or a man?" But the solution of these puzzles is clear even from our previous answers to their questions. Nevertheless, let us right now say what ought to be said summarily by way of reply, so that no opportunity may be left for their cunning.

When they ask whether Mary is a man's mother or God's mother, we must say, "Both," the one by the nature of the thing, the other in virtue of a relation. Mary was a man's mother by nature, since what was in her womb was a man, just as it was also a man who came forth from her womb. But she is God's mother, since God was in the man who was fashioned—not circumscribed in him by nature but existing in him according to the disposition of his will.

Therefore, it is right to say both, but not in the same sense. God the Logos did not, like the man, begin to exist when he was in the womb, for he existed before every creature. Therefore, it is right to say both, and each in an appropriate sense.

And the same answer must be given if they ask, "Was God crucified, or a man?" That is to say, one must answer, "Both, indeed, but not in the same sense." The latter was crucified in the sense that he suffered and was nailed to the cross and was held by the Jews, but the former because he was with him, for the reason we have given.

IX.

The Controversies Leading Up to the Council of Chalcedon

NESTORIUS'S FIRST SERMON AGAINST THE *THEOTOKOS*

The teaching of true religion is the aim of those in the church who are gifted with insight, and the teaching of true religion is the knowledge of providence. That person knows providence, moreover, who knows that God is the guardian of bodies and of souls. Consequently, whoever worships God without knowing this is obviously ignorant of the truth, for "they profess that they know God, but," as it is written, "they deny him by what they do" [Titus 1:16].

Moreover, it is a matter of necessity that the Creator take care of those whom he has created. It is a matter of necessity that the Lord be solicitous for those over whom he rules. It is a matter of necessity that the head of the family be the defender of his household. To the dignity of so great a rule, our own life is not equal.

The Creator God, after all, fashioned me in my mother's womb, and he is the first and supreme surety that in those hidden places of the interior I am kept in existence. I am born—and I discover fountains of milk. I begin to experience a need to cut my food in bits, and discover that I am equipped with knives of a sort in my teeth. I come to maturity, and the creation becomes the source of my wealth, for the earth nourishes me from beneath, and from heaven above the sun is kindled as a lamp for me. The spring season presents me with flowers, the summer offers me the ripe head of grain, the winter brings rains to birth, autumn hangs its gift out on the vine.

What an uneven life we lead, put together as it is of poverty and riches! Yet mortal things could not have continued in being in any other way. Just consider what a protection there is for us in these very circumstances. The decay of grain easily compels the rich to sell it to the needy, from fear of spoilage; and the changeable nature of the grape forces its owner into commerce to avoid damage to his crop. That is why gold is incapable of spoiling and resists the effects of time—the poor man comes to no harm when it is held back. Why do the riches of the prosperous grieve me, if they hold back their gold, while they are forced to sell what nourishes me?

The human race was adorned with ten thousand gifts when it was dignified by a gift which was furthest away and nearest to hand —the Lord's incarnation. Because humanity is the image of the divine nature, but the devil overthrew this image and cast it down into corruption, God grieved over his image as a king might grieve over his statue, and renewed the ruined likeness. Without male seed, he fashioned from the Virgin a nature like Adam's (who was himself formed without male seed) and through a human being brought about the revival of the human race. "Since," Paul says, "death came through a human being, through a human being also came the resurrection of the dead" [1 Cor. 15:21].

Let those people pay attention to these words who, blinded with regard to the dispensation of the Lord's incarnation, "do not understand either the words they employ or the things they are talking about" [1 Tim. 1:7]. I mean those who, as we have now learned, are always inquiring among us now this way and now that: "Is Mary *theotokos*," they say (that is, the bearer or mother of God), "or is she on the contrary *anthrōpotokos*" (that is, the bearer or mother of a human being)?

Does God have a mother? A Greek without reproach introducing mothers for the gods! Is Paul then a liar when he says of the deity of Christ, "without father, without mother, without genealogy" [Heb. 7:3]? Mary, my friend, did not give birth to the Godhead (for "what is born of the flesh is flesh" [John 3:6]). A creature did not produce him who is uncreatable. The Father has not just recently generated God the Logos from the Virgin (for "in the beginning was the Logos," as John [John 1:1] says). A creature did not produce the Creator, rather she gave birth to the human being, the instrument of the Godhead. The Holy Spirit did not create God the Logos (for "what is born of her is of the Holy Spirit" [Matt. 1:20]). Rather, he formed out of the Virgin a temple for God the Logos, a temple in which he dwelt.

Moreover, the incarnate God did not die; he raised up the one in whom he was incarnate. He stooped down to raise up what had collapsed, but he did not fall ("The Lord looked down from heaven over the sons of men" [Ps. 14:2]). Nor, because he stooped to lift up the guilty who had fallen, may he be disparaged as if he himself had sunk to the ground. God saw the ruined nature, and the power of the Godhead took hold of it in its shattered state. God held on to it while himself remaining what he had been, and lifted it up high.

For the sake of an illustration of what is meant, note this: If you want to lift up someone who is lying down, do you not touch body with body and, by joining yourself to the other person, lift up the hurt one while you, joined to him in this fashion, remain what you were? This is the way to think of the mystery of the incarnation. . . .

That is why Paul also says, "who *is* the radiance of his glory" [Heb. 1:3], lest, namely, someone who had heard the words "He *was* in the form of God" [Phil. 2:6] should conjecture that his nature is transitory and has been altered. John, it is true, when describing the shared and mutual eternity of the Logos and the Father, uses these words: "In the beginning was the Logos" [John 1:1]. He does not use the word *is*, he did not say, "In the beginning *is* the Logos, and the Logos *is* with God." No. He said, "In the beginning *was* the Logos, and the Logos *was* with God, and the Logos *was* God." For the question concerned the original subsistence of the being which carried the humanity. Paul, however, recounts all at once everything which happened, that the [divine] being has become incarnate and that the immutability of the incarnate deity is always maintained after the union. That is why, as he writes, he cries out, "Let this mind be in you which was also in Christ Jesus, who being in the form of God . . . emptied himself, taking the form of a slave" [Phil. 2:5–7]. He did not say, "Let this mind be in you which was in God the Logos, who being in the

125

form of God, took the form of a slave." Rather, he takes the term *Christ* to be an expression which signifies the two natures, and without risk he applies to him both the style "form of a slave," which he took, and that of God. The descriptions are different from each other by reason of the mysterious fact that the natures are two in number.

Furthermore, it is not only this—that Christ as God is unaffected by change—which must be proclaimed to Christians but also that he is benevolent, that he takes "the form of a slave" while existing as he was, in order that you may know not only that he was not altered after the union but that he has been revealed as both benevolent and just.

For the sinless death for sinners belongs to his flesh, and it is a gift of inestimable benevolence that he did not spurn a death on behalf of his enemies, for according to Paul, "one will scarcely die for a righteous person" [Rom. 5:7]. Furthermore, to accept the human race by the agency of a human being and to reconcile Adam represents a vast policy of justice. It was just to set free this nature which had offended, now again made pleasing to God, and it is just to absolve the nature, formerly liable to punishment, which had incurred the debt. Humanity owed God an unblamable life lived without complaint, but it fell short in carrying out its duty. Since the soul was stripped of virtues, the passions resulting from its heedlessness drove it hither and thither, and rare were the possessors of piety and virtue—just consider the people who, in the deprived circumstances of that time, seemed or were thought to possess it! Through the whole earth debt was in power ("For all," says Paul, "have sinned, and fall short of the glory of God" [Rom. 3:23]), and the consequences of sin were growing.

What, then, of the Lord Christ? Perceiving that the human race was tied up in its sins and unworthy of restoration, he did not dissolve the debt by an order, lest mercy violate justice. And the apostle Paul is a witness of this when he exclaims, "Christ, whom God set forth as an expiation through faith in his blood to demonstrate his justice" [Rom. 3:25]—that mercy, he means, may be shown to be just and not something bestowed without judgment here and there and how you please.

Consequently, Christ assumed the person of the debt-ridden

nature and by its mediation paid the debt back as a son of Adam, for it was obligatory that the one who dissolved the debt come from the same race as he who had once contracted it. The debt had its start from a woman, and the remission had its start from a woman.

But learn what the nature of the debt was, in order that you may learn what the repayment was. Adam became liable to punishment because of food. Christ releases him from this punishment by fasting in the desert, by spurning the devil's counsel about the refreshment that food brings. Adam fell into the guilt of seeking divinity for himself in opposition to God, since he had heard the devil say, "You will be as gods" [Gen. 3:5], and had quickly snatched the bait. But Christ releases him by his answer to the devil when the latter made a promise of power (for he said to him, "I will give you everything if you will fall down and worship me" [Matt. 4:9]). Christ himself rejected the devil's words: "Depart, Satan; you shall worship the Lord God and you shall serve him alone" [Matt. 4:10]. Because of his disobedience in the case of a tree, Adam was under sentence of punishment; Christ made up for this debt, too, "having become obedient" [Phil. 2:8] on a tree. That is why Paul said, "He took away the handwritten bond of our sins, which stood against us, nailing it to the cross" [Col. 2:14]. Moreover, the one who made restoration on our behalf is Christ, for in him our nature discharges its debt. He had assumed a person of the same nature [as ours], whose passions were removed by his passion, since, as Paul put it, "We have redemption in his blood" [Eph. 1:7].

Now see our nature, in God's company in Christ, pleading its case against the devil and employing the following valid arguments. "I am oppressed by wrong, O most just judge. The wicked devil attacks me; he uses my powerlessness against me in a manifest assertion of unjust power. Be it so that he handed the former Adam over to death because he was the occasion of [Adam's] sinning; and now the Second Adam, whom you have formed out of a virgin—for what offense, O King, has he crucified him? What is the reason that he has hanged thieves together with him? Why is it that he who did no sin, neither was guile found in his mouth, is reckoned with the transgressors [1 Pet. 2:22; Isa. 53:12]? Or is it

127

possible that his execrable intent is not obvious? He is openly envious of me, Lord, in my role as your image. Without any occasion, he attacks me and attempts to overthrow me. But show yourself a just judge on my behalf. You have been angry at me by reason of Adam's transgression. I beseech you, on his behalf, to be favorable, if it be the case that you have joined to you an Adam who is without sin. Be it so that on account of the former Adam you have handed me over to corruption; on this one's account, make me partake of incorruption. Both of them have my nature. As I shared in the death of the former, so I shall become a participant in the immortal life of the second.

"I am supported by indubitable and unassailable arguments. I triumph over adversaries on every hand. If he brings a charge against me because of the corruption which became mine because of Adam, I shall cross it out from the opposite side by appeal to the life of him who did no sin. And if he accuses me on the basis of Adam's disobedience, I will render him the condemned one on the basis of the Second Adam's obedience. Leading this triumph in virtue of his victory over the devil, Christ says, 'Now is the judgment of this world, now the prince of this world is cast out'" [John 12:31]."

Just as the devil held the protoplast's sin against his whole posterity and sustained the original charge, so too, when our nature had in Christ come into possession of the guiltless firstfruits of its total body, it struggled against the devil and conquered, by means of the very weapons which the adversary had used previously. If the devil urges the earlier causes of our condemnation on the basis of what Adam did, it pleads against him with complete justification the blameless origin of its firstfruits in Christ. Paul says, "It is Christ, who died for our sins, and more, who rose from the dead and is at the right hand of God, who also intervenes on our behalf" [Rom. 8:34]. Our nature, having been put on by Christ like a garment, intervenes on our behalf, being entirely free from all sin and contending by appeal to its blameless origin, just as the Adam who was formed earlier brought punishment upon his race by reason of his sin. This was the opportunity which belonged to the assumed man, as a human being to dissolve, by means of the flesh, that corruption which arose by means of the flesh. The third-day burial belonged to this man, not to the deity. His feet were fastened down by nails; he is the one whom the Holy Spirit formed in the womb. It was about this flesh that the Lord said to the Jews, "Destroy this temple and in three days I will raise it up" [John 2:19].

Am I the only one who calls Christ "twofold"? Does he not call himself both a destroyable temple and God who raises it up? And if it was God who was destroyed—and let that blasphemy be shifted to the head of Arius!—the Lord would have said, "Destroy this God and in three days I will raise him up." If God died when consigned to the grave, the Gospel saying "Why do you seek to kill me, a man, who have spoken truth to you?" [John 8:40] is meaningless.

But Christ is not a mere man, O slanderer! No, he is at once God and man. If he were God alone, he would have needed, O Apollinaris, to say, "Why do you seek to destroy me, who am God, who have spoken the truth to you?" What, in fact, he says is, "Why do you seek to kill me, a man?" This is he who is crowned with the crown of thorns. This is he who says, "My God, my God, why have you forsaken me?" [Matt. 27:46]. This is he who suffered a death of three days' duration. But I worship this one together with the Godhead because he is a sharer in the divine authority; "for let it be apparent, men and brothers," says the Scripture, "that the remission of sins is preached to us through Christ" [Acts 13:38].

I adore him as the instrument of the Lord's goodness, for he says, "Be kind and merciful to one another, even as God has given to us in Christ" [Eph. 4:32]. I honor him as the meeting place of God's counsels, for "I want you to have knowledge of the mystery of God the Father and Christ, in whom all the treasures of wisdom and knowledge are hidden" [Col. 2:1-3]. I receive him as the "form" which makes promise on God's behalf for us. "He who sent me," he says, "is true, and I speak the things which I have heard from him" [John 8:26]. I bless him as the pledge of peace; "for he," it says, "is our peace, who made the two one, and destroyed the wall of division in between, enmities in his flesh" [Eph. 2:14]. I worship him as the expiation of divine wrath: "Christ," he says, "God set forth as an expiation for faith through faith in his blood" [Rom. 3:25]. I love and revere him as the beginning of immortality for mortals; "for he," it says, "is the head of his body, the church, who is the beginning, the firstborn from the dead" [Col. 1:18]. I embrace him as the mirror of the resplendent deity; for "God," it says, "was in Christ reconciling the world to himself" [2 Cor. 5:19]. I adore him as the living glory of the King; for "constituted in the form of God, he emptied himself, taking the form of a slave, and was found in the condition of a human being" [Phil. 2:6–7]. I praise him as the hand of God which snatches me out of the hand of death for life; for "when I have been lifted up," he says, "from the earth, then I will draw all to myself" [John 12:32]. And who it is who is exalted the faithful scribe tells us when he says, "For this he said to show by what death he would die" [John 12:33]. I marvel at him as the door through which one enters upon divine things; for "I am the door," he says; "anyone who enters through me will be set free and will go in and go out and will find a dwelling" [John 10:9]. I worship him as the image of the all-sovereign deity; for "God exalted him and gave him the name above every name, so that at the name of Jesus every knee shall bow, of things in heaven and things on earth and things under the earth, and every tongue confess that Jesus Christ is Lord" [Phil. 2:9–11]. I revere the one who is borne because of the one who carries him, and I worship the one I see because of the one who is hidden. God is undivided from the one who appears, and therefore I do not divide the honor of that which is not divided. I divide the natures, but I unite the worship.

Attend to what is said here. That which was formed in the womb is not in itself God. That which was created by the Spirit was not in itself God. That which was buried in the tomb was not in itself God. If that were the case, we should manifestly be worshipers of a human being and worshipers of the dead. But since God is within the one who was assumed, the one who was assumed is styled God because of the one who assumed him. That is why the demons shudder at the mention of the crucified flesh; they know that God has been joined to the crucified flesh, even though he has not shared its suffering.

Therefore also this one who appeared to people's sight will come as judge, because he is joined to omnipotent deity. "For at that time," it says, "the sign of the Son of man will appear in the sky, and they will see the Son of man coming on the clouds of the sky with power and great glory" [Matt. 24:30]. Just as a king whose victory has been won appears in his cities with the arms with which he conquered the enemy in war and wants himself to be seen in their company, so the King who is Lord of all things will come to his creatures with a cross and with flesh, to be seen with these arms by which he overcame impiety. And with almighty power he will judge the earth in the form of a human being, in accordance with Paul's proclamation: "The times of ignorance God overlooked, but now he commands all persons everywhere to repent, since he has determined a day on which he will judge the world through a man, in whom he determined to give an assurance to all by raising him from the dead" [Acts 17:30–31]. . . .

God formed . . . so let us begin to tremble at the Lord's incarnation, speaking in divine terms of the "form" which received God (*theodochos*) together with the divine Logos, as the inseparable image of the divine authority, as the image of the hidden Judge. We confess both and adore them as one, for the duality of the natures is one on account of the unity. Hear Paul proclaiming both the eternity of the Only Begotten's deity and the recent birth of the humanity, and the fact that the dignity of the association or conjunction has been made one. "Jesus Christ," he says, "is the same yesterday and today and forever" [Heb. 13:8]. Amen.

CYRIL OF ALEXANDRIA'S SECOND LETTER TO NESTORIUS

Cyril to his most reverend and God-beloved
fellow minister Nestorius.
Greetings in the Lord.

Certain persons, I learn, continue to chatter in your piety's presence to the detriment of my character. What is more, they do this often, taking special care to appear at gatherings of officials and supposing, no doubt, that they may contrive to give you pleasure. What they say is ill-advised, since they have not been unjustly dealt with in any way. On the contrary, they have been convicted, and that rightfully—one because he did hurt to the blind and the poor, one because he threatened his mother with a sword, and the third, in the company of a female slave, stole someone else's gold and has always possessed a reputation of the sort one would not be found attributing to one's worst enemies. In any case, the speech of people of this kind does not mean much to me, for I do not stretch the limits of my littleness to the point where I exceed my Lord and Master, or indeed the fathers. It is impossible to evade the mischief of the wicked, no matter how one conducts one's life.

Those men, however, "whose mouth is full of cursing and bitterness" [Rom. 3:14], will give their account to the Judge of all. I, for my part, shall again turn to the matters which properly concern me. I shall even now remind you, as my brother in Christ, to make the balance of your teaching and your thinking about the faith as safe as possible for the laity, and also to keep in mind that to cause even one of these little ones who believe in Christ to stumble wins implacable wrath.

If, though, there should be a great number of people who are distressed, surely we stand in need of all our skill, at once for the sake of removing the scandal in a sensible fashion, and for the sake of opening up the healthful teaching of the faith for those who seek the truth. This, moreover, will be done most rightly if, as we encounter the teachings of the holy fathers, we are eager to make much of them, and if, "testing ourselves," as it is written, "to see if we are in the faith" [2 Cor. 13:5], we form our own ideas in accordance with their correct and unexceptionable opinions.

Now the great and holy synod stated that the unique Son himself—naturally begotten out of God the Father, true God out of true God, light out of light, through whom the Father made everything that exists—descended, was enfleshed, became human, rose on the third day, and ascended into the heavens.

It is incumbent on us to be true to these statements and teachings and to comprehend what is meant by saying that the Logos from God took flesh and became human. We do not say that the Logos became flesh by having his nature changed, nor for that matter that he was transformed into a complete human being composed out of soul and body. On the contrary, we say that in an unspeakable and incomprehensible way, the Logos united to himself, in his hypostasis, flesh enlivened by a rational soul, and in this way became a human being and has been designated "Son of man." He did not become a human being simply by an act of will or "good pleasure," any more than he did so by merely taking on a person.

Furthermore, we say that while the natures which were brought together into a true unity were different, there is nevertheless, because of the unspeakable and unutterable convergence into unity, one Christ and one Son out of the two. This is the sense in which it is said that, although he existed and was born from the Father before the ages, he was also born of a woman in his flesh. The idea is not that he found the beginning of his existence inside the holy Virgin, nor is it that he necessarily stood in need of a second birth through her in addition to his birth from the Father, for it is at once stupid and pointless to assert that one who exists prior to every age, coeternal with the Father, is in need of a second way of coming into being. Since, however, the Logos was born of a woman after he had, "for us and for our salvation," united human reality hypostatically to himself, he is said on this ground to have had a fleshly birth. It is not the case that first of all an ordinary human being was born of the holy Virgin and that the Logos descended upon him subsequently. On the contrary, since the union took place in the very womb, he is said to have undergone a fleshly birth by making his own the birth of the flesh which belonged to him.

We assert that this is the way in which he suffered and rose from the dead. It is not that the Logos of God suffered in his own nature, being overcome by stripes or nail-piercing or any of the other injuries; for the divine, since it is incorporeal, is impassible. Since, however, the body that had become his own underwent suffering, he is—once again—said to have suffered these things for our sakes, for the impassible One was within the suffering body. Moreover, we reason in exactly the same way in the case of his dying. God's Logos is by nature immortal and incorruptible and Life and Life-giver, but since, as Paul says, "by the grace of God" his very own body "tasted death on behalf of every person" [Heb. 2:9], he himself is said to have suffered this death which came about on our account. It is not that he actually experienced death as far as anything which touches his [divine] nature is concerned; to think that would be insanity. Rather it is that, as I said earlier, his flesh tasted death.

So also, when his flesh was raised, the resurrection is also said to be his, not as if he fell into corruption (which God forbid!) but because, again, his body was raised.

This is the sense in which we confess one Christ and Lord. We do not worship a human being in conjunction with the Logos, lest the appearance of a division creep in by reason of that phrase "in conjunction with." No, we worship one and the same, because the body of the Logos is not alien to him but accompanies him even as he is enthroned with the Father. Again, it is not that there are two Sons enthroned together but rather that there is one, on account of the [Logos'] union with the flesh. If, however, we set aside this union in the order of the hypostasis as if it were pointless or unseemly, we fall into the assertion of two Sons, for it becomes necessary to divide the integral whole and to say that on the one hand there is a proper human being who is dignified with the title of "Son," while on the other hand there is the proper Logos of God, who possesses by nature both the name and the exercise of sonship.

Therefore, the one Lord Jesus Christ must not be divided into two Sons. The correct expression of the faith is not assisted by taking this line, even when some allege that there is a union of persons, for Scripture says not that the Logos united to himself the person of a human being but that he became flesh. And for the Logos to become flesh is nothing other than for him to "share in flesh and blood as we do" [Heb. 2:14], to make his own a body from among us, and to be born of woman as a human being. He did not depart from his divine status or cease to be born of the Father; he continued to be what he was, even in taking on flesh. This is what the teaching of the correct faith everywhere proclaims. And this is how we shall find the holy fathers conceived things. Accordingly, they boldly called the holy Virgin "God's mother" [*theotokos*], not because the nature of the Logos or the deity took the start of its existence in the holy Virgin but because the holy body which was born of her, possessed as it was of a rational soul, and to which the Logos was hypostatically united, is said to have had a fleshly birth.

These things I write you now out of the love which is in Christ, and I exhort you as a brother and "charge you before the Christ and the elect angels" [1 Tim. 5:21] to think and teach these things in company with us, so that the peace of the churches may be preserved and that the bond of like-mindedness and love may continue unbroken for God's priests.

NESTORIUS'S SECOND LETTER
TO CYRIL

To his most reverend and God-fearing
fellow minister Cyril
Nestorius sends greeting in the Lord.

The rebukes which your astonishing letter brings against us I forgive. What it deserves is a healing generosity of spirit and the reply which comes to it at the proper time by way of actual deeds. This, though, does not permit silence, for if silence be kept, great danger is involved. On this account, standing against your prolixity as far as may be possible, I will attempt to make my exposition brief and maintain my distaste for obscure and indigestible haranguing.

I shall begin from Your Charity's all-wise utterances, having first quoted them expressly. Here, then, are some statements from the astonishing teaching of your letter.

"The great and holy synod stated that the unique Son himself —naturally begotten out of God the Father, true God out of true God, light out of light, through whom the Father made everything that exists—descended, was enfleshed, became human, suffered, rose." These are Your Piety's words, and you doubtless acknowledge them as yours.

Now hear our brotherly exhortation on behalf of true religion, in accordance with the testimony which that great one, Paul, gave to

Timothy his friend. "Give heed to reading, to exhortation, to teaching . . . for by doing this you will save both yourself and your hearers" [1 Tim. 4:13–16].

What does this phrase "give heed" mean to me? That in reading the doctrine of those holy men superficially, you did not recognize the excusable want of perception in your judgment that they assert the passibility of the Logos who is coeternal with God. So if it seems right, examine what was said more closely, and you will discover that the divine chorus of the Fathers did not say that the coessential Godhead is passible or that the Godhead which is coeternal with the Father has only just been born, or that he who has raised up the temple which was destroyed has [himself] risen. And if you will give me your attention for the sake of brotherly correction, I will explain to you the utterances of those holy men and deliver you from calumnies against them and, through them, against the Holy Scriptures.

"We also believe," they said, "in our Lord Jesus Christ, his only-begotten Son." Observe how they first of all establish, as foundations, the titles which are common to the deity and the humanity—"Lord" and "Jesus" and "Christ" and "Only Begotten" and "Son"—and then build on them the teaching about his becoming human and his passion and resurrection, in order that, since the titles which signify and are common to both natures are set in the foreground, the things which pertain to the sonship and lordship are not divided and the things peculiar to the natures within the unitary sonship do not get endangered by the suggestion of a confusion.

Paul himself was their instructor in this matter. He refers to the divine act of becoming human, and since he is about to add mention of the passion, he first posits the title "Christ," the title which, as I said earlier, is common to the two natures, and then introduces words that are appropriate to the two natures. What does he say? "Let this mind be in you which was also in Christ Jesus, who being in the form of God, did not think equality with God something to be snatched at, but"—to shorten the quotation—"became obedient to death, even the death of the Cross" [Phil. 2:5–8]. Since he was about to recall the death, lest anyone for that reason suppose that God the Logos is passible, he inserts the word "Christ," because it is the term which signifies the impassible and the passible essence in one unitary person, with the result that Christ is without risk called both impassible and passible—impassible in the Godhead but passible in the nature of the body.

I could say many things about this—first that those holy fathers spoke not of birth when they were thinking of God's saving dispensation but of coming to be in a human being—but I realize that my opening promise of brevity constrains my speech and turns me to your Charity's second head. In this connection I commended the distinction of natures in accordance with the special character of humanity and deity, the conjunction of these natures in one person, the denial that the Logos has need of a second birth from a woman, and the confession that the Godhead is not susceptible to passion. Certainly such beliefs are most truly orthodox and contrary to the evil teachings of all the heresies about the Lord's natures. If, however, the remainder conveys some hidden wisdom, incapable of being grasped by the hearing of its readers, that is for your acuteness to understand. To me it seemed right to center interest on the primary issues, for I do not see how he reintroduced as passible and newly created one who had first been proclaimed as impassible and incapable of a second birth—as if the qualities which attach naturally to God the Logos are corrupted by his conjunction with his temple; or as if people consider it a small thing that the sinless temple, which is also inseparable from the divine nature, underwent birth and death on behalf of sinners; or as if the Lord's saying, cried out to the Jews, is not worthy of belief: "Destroy this temple and in three days I will raise it" [John 2:19]. He did not say, "Destroy my divinity and in three days I will raise it."

Wishing again to expand on this theme too, I am brought to a halt by the recollection of my promise. Nevertheless, I must speak, while using brevity.

Everywhere in Holy Scripture, whenever mention is made of the saving dispensation of the Lord, what is conveyed to us is the birth and suffering not of the deity but of the humanity of Christ, so that by a more exact manner of speech the holy Virgin is called Mother of Christ, not Mother of God. Listen to these words of the

Gospels: "The book of the birth of Jesus Christ, son of David, son of Abraham" [Matt. 1:1]. It is obvious that the son of David was not the divine Logos. And hear another witness, if it seems right: "Jacob begat Joseph, the husband of Mary, of whom was born Jesus who is called Christ" [Matt. 1:16]. Consider another voice bearing witness for us: "The birth of Jesus Christ was on this wise, for when his mother Mary was betrothed to Joseph, she was discovered to have conceived in her womb by the Holy Spirit" [Matt. 1:18]. Shall I suppose that the deity of the Only Begotten is a creature of the Spirit? And what shall it mean that "the mother of Jesus was there" [John 2:1]? And again, "with Mary the mother of Jesus" [Acts 1:14]; and "that which is born in her is of the Holy Spirit" [Matt. 1:20]; and "Take the child and his mother and flee into Egypt" [Matt. 2:13]; and "concerning his Son, who was born of the seed of David according to the flesh" [Rom. 1:3]; and again this, concerning the passion: "God sent his Son in the likeness of sinful flesh, and because of sin, and condemned sin in the flesh" [Rom. 8:3]; and again, "Christ died for our sins" [1 Cor. 15:3]; and "Christ suffered in the flesh" [1 Pet. 4:1]; and "This is," not my deity, but "my body which is broken for you" [1 Cor. 11:24]— and thousands of other statements warning the human race not to think that the deity of the Son is a new thing, or susceptible to bodily passion, but rather the flesh which is united to the nature of the Godhead.

That is why Christ calls himself both Lord and son of David. He says, "'What do you think about the Christ? Whose son is he?' They say to him, 'David's.' Jesus answered and said to them, 'How then does David, speaking in the Spirit, call him Lord, saying, "The Lord said to my Lord, 'Sit on my right hand'"'?" [Matt. 22:42–44], because he is entirely the son of David according to the flesh but Lord according to the deity. The body therefore is the temple of the Son's deity, and a temple united to it by a complete and divine conjunction, so that the nature of the deity associates itself with the things belonging to the body, and the body is acknowledged to be noble and worthy of the wonders related in the Gospels.

138

To attribute also to him, in the name of this association, the characteristics of the flesh that has been conjoined with him—I mean birth and suffering and death—is, my brother, either the work of a mind which truly errs in the fashion of the Greeks or that of a mind diseased with the insane heresy of Arius and Apollinaris and the others. Those who are thus carried away with the idea of this association are bound, because of it, to make the divine Logos have a part in being fed with milk and participate to some degree in growth and stand in need of angelic assistance because of his fearfulness at the time of the passion. I say nothing about circumcision and sacrifice and tears and hunger, which, being joined with him, belong properly to the flesh as things which happened for our sake. These things are taken falsely when they are put off on the deity, and they become the occasion of just condemnation for us who perpetrate the falsehood.

These are the teachings of the holy fathers. This is the message of the divine Scriptures. This is the way in which one speaks theologically both of the things which belong to God's love for the human race and of the things which belong to his majesty. "Be diligent in these things, concern yourself with them, that your progress may be evident to all" [1 Tim. 4:15], says Paul to everyone.

It is right for you, since you are withstood, to give thought to those who are scandalized. And thanks be to your soul, mindful as it is of divine things, giving thought to people here as well. Know, however, that you have been misled by the clergy of your own persuasion, by those deposed here by the holy synod because they thought like Manichaeans. The affairs of the church make progress in every quarter, and the laity are increasing at such a rate, through the grace of God, that those who see the multitudes cry out the words of the prophet, "The earth shall be filled with the knowledge of the Lord as a great water covers the sea" [Isa. 11:9]. Also, the affairs of the emperors are in a state of overflowing joy because the teaching has been illumined. And—in order that I may bring my letter to an end—may people discover that amongst us, where all heresies hateful to God and the correct teaching of the church are concerned, this word has been fulfilled: "The house of Saul went on and became weaker and the house of David went on and became stronger" [2 Sam. 3:1].

This is our counsel, given as from brother to brother. "But if anyone seems contentious," as Paul cried out for our sakes to such a person, "we have no such custom, neither the churches of God" [1 Cor. 11:16]. I and all who are with me send many greetings to the whole brotherhood of your company. May you continue in good health and praying for us, O most entirely honored and beloved of God!

CYRIL'S LETTER TO JOHN OF ANTIOCH

*To my Lord, well-beloved brother
and fellow minister John,
Cyril sends greeting in the Lord.*

"Let the heavens rejoice and let the earth exult" [Ps. 96:11], for the "middle wall of division" [Eph. 2:14] has been destroyed and an end has been put to grieving and the cause of all discord has been taken away, since Christ, the Savior of us all, has awarded peace to all his churches. What is more, the pious and God-beloved emperors have summoned us to this peace. They have become the noblest followers of the piety of their forebears, and they guard the correct faith sure and undisturbed in their own souls. Further, they have a special concern for the holy churches, so that they may have open acclaim for eternity and cause their dominion to appear most glorious. To them the Lord of the heavenly powers distributes good things with a liberal hand and enables them to prevail over their enemies and graces them with victory. There could be no lying with the one who said, "I live, says the Lord, because I will give glory to those who glorify me" [1 Sam. 2:30].

When, therefore, my lord Paul, my God-beloved brother and fellow minister, arrived in Alexandria, we were filled with pleasure —and with good reason, since a person of such quality was acting as mediator and chose to experience undue labor in order that he might overcome the envy of the devil and reunite things that had been divided and, when he had removed the occasion of stumbling which had been cast between us, might crown with peace both your churches and mine. In what way they were divided, it is superfluous to say. I judge it best to think and speak the things that belong to a time of peace.

So we took pleasure in our discussion with the aforementioned God-beloved man. He probably suspected that he would have to struggle greatly to persuade us that it was necessary to join the churches together for the sake of peace and for the sake of stopping the laughter of the heterodox, not to mention blunting the point of the devil's determination. But he discovered people so readily disposed to this end as to require no trouble at all. We remembered the Savior's words "My peace I give to you, my peace I leave to you" [John 14:27]. And we have been taught to say in our prayers, "O Lord our God, give us peace, for you have given us everything," for if someone becomes a sharer in the peace which is abundantly given by God, he has no need of any good thing. We have been fully assured that the separation of the churches was superfluous and had no real occasion, since the God-beloved bishop Paul has presented a document containing a sincere confession of the faith and has certified that it was drawn up by Your Holiness and the most pious bishops of that place. This is what the document says, and it is inserted in our letter word for word:

"Without making any addition at all to the faith set forth by the holy fathers at Nicaea, we must say in short compass how we think and speak concerning the virgin Mother of God and the manner in which the only-begotten Son of God became a human being—not by way of supplement but in the form of a full exposition, as we have always possessed it, having received it from the divine Scriptures and the tradition of the holy fathers. As we have just said, it is sufficient both for the knowledge of the whole of true religion and for the exclusion of all heretical wrong thinking, and we will state it, not hazarding impossibilities but with confession of our own weakness, shutting out those who wish to charge that we are looking into matters beyond human understanding.

"Therefore we confess that our Lord Jesus Christ, the only-begotten Son of God, is complete God and complete human being with a rational soul and a body. He was born from the Father before the ages, as to his deity, but at the end of the days the same one was born, for our sake and the sake of our salvation, from Mary the Virgin, as to his humanity. This same one is coessential with the Father, as to his deity, and coessential with us, as to his humanity, for a union of two natures has occurred, as a consequence of which we confess one Christ, one Son, one Lord. In accordance with this concept of the unconfused union, we confess that the holy Virgin is Mother of God, because the divine Logos was made flesh and became a human being and from the moment of conception itself united to himself the temple which he took from her.

"And as to the things said about the Lord in the Gospels and apostolic writings, we know that theologians make some common, as applying to one person, and divide others, as applying to the two natures, and teach that some are appropriate to God in accordance with Christ's deity, while others are lowly in accordance with his humanity."

Having read these your holy words, and finding that we ourselves think in the same way—for there is "one Lord, one faith, one baptism" [Eph. 4:5]—we gave glory to God the Savior of all, and we rejoiced with one another that your churches and ours have a faith in agreement with that of the inspired Scriptures and the tradition of the holy fathers.

But when we heard that certain persons with a disposition to be censorious were buzzing about in the fashion of savage wasps and spewing out wicked allegations against me, to the effect that I assert that the holy body of Christ was sent down from heaven and did not come from the holy Virgin, I thought it necessary to address a few words to them on this subject.

Mindless ones! People who know only how to make false accusations! How were you brought to such a state of mind and infected with such foolishness? You really have an obligation to understand clearly that almost the whole of the struggle on account of the faith was waged because of our conviction that the holy Virgin is the Mother of God. But if we assert that it was from heaven and not from her that there came the holy body of Christ the Savior of us all, how can she still be thought of as Mother of God? To whom did she give birth if it is not true that she bore Emmanuel in his flesh? So let those who have talked this nonsense about me be objects of ridicule, for the blessed prophet Isaiah does not lie when he says, "Behold, a virgin shall conceive and bear a son, and they shall call his name Emmanuel, which means 'God with us'" [Matt. 1:23; cf. Isa. 7:14], and the holy Gabriel tells the simple truth when he says to the blessed Virgin, "Do not be afraid, Mary, for you have found favor with God; and behold, you will conceive in your womb and you will bear a son, and you will call his name Jesus" [Luke 1:30–31], "for he will save his people from their sins" [Matt. 1:21].

But when we say that our Lord Jesus Christ is from heaven and from above, we do not mean that his holy body was brought down from heaven. Rather we follow the holy Paul, who cried out plainly, "The first human being is of earth, earthy; the second human being is [the Lord] from heaven" [1 Cor. 15:47]. And we remember that the Savior himself said, "No one has gone up into heaven except he who came down from heaven, the Son of man" [John 3:13]—even though, as far as his flesh was concerned, he was born of the holy Virgin, as I said earlier. Since, however, the divine Logos who came down from above and from heaven "emptied himself and took the form of a slave" [Phil. 2:7] and was also called "Son of man" while remaining what he was (that is, God; for he is unchangeable and unalterable by nature), he is said to have come down because he is now conceived to be one with his own flesh, and so he is called "the human being from heaven," the same one being complete in his deity and complete in his humanity and understood to exist in one person. There is one Lord Jesus Christ, even though we do not ignore the difference of the natures out of which we say the inexpressible union has been made.

As for those who say that God has been "mixed" or "confused" or "blended" with his flesh, let Your Holiness make it his business to silence them, for it is likely that people are repeating this about me, as though I have thought or said it. But I have been so far from thinking any such thing that I count all those as madmen who think that "a shadow of turning" [James 1:17] can attach to the divine nature, for it remains what it always is and has not been altered. Indeed, it could never have been altered or ever be susceptible to change. Furthermore, we all confess that the divine Logos is impassible, even though, since he himself carries out the mystery [of salvation], he is seen to attribute to himself the passions that occur in his own flesh. The all-wise Peter says, "Christ suffered on our account in the flesh" [1 Pet. 4:1] and not in the nature of the unutterable deity. In order that he may be believed to be Savior of the universe, Christ refers the passions of his own flesh—as I have said—to himself by means of an appropriation which occurs for the sake of our salvation. This sort of thing was announced beforehand by the voice of the prophet (who speaks in the person of Christ): "I have given my back to the whips, my cheeks to blows, and I have not turned my face away from the shame of spitting" [Isa. 50:6].

Let Your Holiness be persuaded and let no one else doubt that we follow the views of the holy fathers on every point—especially those of our blessed and universally praised father Athanasius—and absolutely decline to be carried outside of them in any respect. I would also have furnished you with many sayings of theirs and so lent credence to my words by theirs, but I was fearful about the length of this document and did not want to become in any way boring on that account.

We do not permit the faith or the symbol of the faith defined by our holy fathers assembled in their day in Nicaea to be shaken by anyone, and we do not trust ourselves or others to change a word of what was laid down there, or to depart from a single syllable of it; for we remember the one who said, "Do not alter the everlasting boundaries which your fathers set" [Prov. 22:28]. It was not they who were speaking, but the Spirit of God the Father, who proceeds out of him without being alien to the Son in essence. Furthermore, the words of the holy mystagogues support us, for in the Acts of the Apostles it is written; "Having come to Mysia, they tried to travel into Bithynia, and the Spirit of Jesus did not permit them" [Acts 16:7]. And the holy Paul writes: "But those who are in the flesh cannot please God; but you are not in the flesh but in the

Spirit, if the Spirit of God dwells in you. But if a person does not have the Spirit of Christ, that person does not belong to him" [Rom. 8:8–9].

When certain people who are in the habit of corrupting correct teachings pervert my words to meanings that please them, Your Holiness should not be amazed. You are aware that even the adherents of heresies collect evidences for their own errors out of the inspired Scriptures and corrupt with their own evil interpretations what has been said correctly through the Holy Spirit.

But since we have learned that some people have issued a corrupted text of the letter which our universally praised father Athanasius wrote, with orthodox meaning, to the blessed Epictetus, with the result that harm has been done to many, we thought, on this account, that it would be something useful and necessary for the brothers, and we have sent Your Holiness duplicates of ancient copies, which originate here and are correct.

May the Lord keep you, honored brother, in good health and praying for us.

POPE LEO I'S LETTER TO FLAVIAN OF CONSTANTINOPLE

(1) I have read Your Charity's letter, with some amazement at the delay in its arrival. After reviewing the record of the bishops' actions, I can now grasp the nature of the outrage which had arisen in your midst against the integrity of the faith, and whatever had seemed obscure is revealed.

Your letter shows that Eutyches, who seemed, from his title of presbyter, to be worthy of esteem, is an extremely foolish and altogether ignorant man. What the prophet said is true in his case also: "He did not wish to learn in order that he might act for the best, in his bed he pondered iniquity" [Ps. 35:4 LXX]. What could be more iniquitous than to dabble in irreverence and to refuse deference to people who are wiser and better instructed than ourselves? This, however, is just the kind of folly people fall into when, in the face of some obscurity which prevents their grasping the truth, they turn to themselves and not to the voices of the prophets, the letters of the apostles, or the authority of the evangelists. The result is that since they have not been students of the truth, they are teachers of error, for what can a person have learned from the sacred pages of the Old and New Testaments when he does not even understand the opening phrases of the creed? What is declared all the world over by the voice of every single candidate for rebirth, this elderly man does not even yet understand in his heart.

(2) Even if, therefore, he did not know what to think about the incarnation of God's Word, and even if he was not willing to work through the whole breadth of the Holy Scriptures in order to gain the light of understanding, he might at any rate have paid careful attention to that shared and indivisible confession in which the universal body of believers professes belief in "God the omnipotent Father" and in "Jesus Christ his unique Son, our Lord, who was born of the Holy Spirit and Mary the Virgin."

By these three assertions, almost all the devices of the heretics are cast down, for when it is believed that God is both omnipotent and Father, it is shown that the Son is coeternal with him, as one who differs from the Father in no respect. After all, he is "God from God," omnipotent from omnipotent. He was begotten as coeternal from the eternal—not later in time or inferior in power or dissimilar in splendor or different in essence. And in truth it is this very same being, this only and eternal Child of the eternal Begetter, who was born "of the Holy Spirit and Mary the Virgin."

This birth in time in no way detracted from that divine and eternal birth and in no way added anything to it. Its entire meaning was worked out in the restoration of humanity, which had been led astray. It came about so that death might be conquered and that the devil, who once exercised death's sovereignty, might by its power be destroyed, for we would not be able to overcome the author of sin and of death unless he whom sin could not stain nor death hold took on our nature and made it his own. So he was conceived by the Holy Spirit within the womb of his virgin mother, and she was as much a virgin when she gave him birth as she was at his conception.

But if Eutyches could not, from this purest source of Christian faith, derive a sound understanding of it—because a blindness peculiar to himself obscured the brightness of evident truth—he might have submitted himself to the teaching of the Gospels. In the face of Matthew's words "The book of the generation of Jesus Christ, the son of David, the son of Abraham" [Matt. 1:1], he might have sought further instruction from the proclamation of the apostle. And when he read in Romans, "Paul, a slave of Jesus Christ, called as an apostle, set apart for the gospel of God, which he had promised earlier through his prophets in the Holy Scriptures, concerning his Son, who in the order of the flesh came to be for him from the seed of David" [Rom. 1:1-3], he might have applied his reverent attention to the pages of the prophets. And when he had come across God's promise to Abraham "In your seed all nations shall be blessed" [Gen. 12:3], lest he have doubts about the meaning of that word "seed," he might have paid attention to the apostle's words "The promises were given to Abraham and to his 'seed.' He does not say 'seeds,' as if referring to more than one. Rather, as if referring to a single 'seed,' he says 'and to your seed'—and that means Christ" [Gal. 3:16]. He might also have listened to Isaiah with interior understanding when the prophet says, "Behold, a virgin shall conceive in her womb and shall give birth to a Son, and they shall call his name 'Emmanuel,' which means 'God with us'" [Matt. 1:23; cf. Isa. 7:14]. And he might have read with faithful heart the words of the same prophet: "A child is born to us, a son is given to us, whose power is upon his shoulder; and they shall call his name 'Angel of Great Counsel,' 'Wonderful Counselor,' 'Strong God,' 'Prince of Peace,' 'Father of the Coming Age'" [Isa. 9:6].

Furthermore, Eutyches might have refrained from speaking deceptively and asserting that "the Word was made flesh" in the sense that Christ, after his birth of the Virgin, possessed the form of a human being but not the reality of his mother's body. Is it possible that the reason he thought our Lord Jesus Christ was not of our nature is that the angel which was sent to the blessed, ever-virgin Mary said, "The Holy Spirit will come upon you and the power of the Most High will overshadow you, and therefore what will be born of you will be called holy, the Son of God" [Luke

1:35]—as if because virginal conception is something God effects, the flesh of the child conceived was not taken from the nature of the woman who conceived it?

That singularly wonderful and wonderfully singular birth must not be understood in such a way as to suggest that the novelty of the method by which the child was produced entailed destruction of the characteristics of the human race. It was the Holy Spirit who made the Virgin fertile, but the substantive reality of the body was derived from her body; so, "since Wisdom was building herself a house" [Prov. 9:1], "the Word became flesh and dwelt among us" [John 1:14].

(3) Since, therefore, the characteristic properties of both natures and substances are kept intact and come together in one person, lowliness is taken on by majesty, weakness by power, mortality by eternity, and the nature which cannot be harmed is united to the nature which suffers, in order that the debt which our condition involves may be discharged. In this way, as our salvation requires, one and the same mediator between God and human beings, the human being who is Jesus Christ, can at one and the same time die in virtue of the one nature and, in virtue of the other, be incapable of death. That is why true God was born in the integral and complete nature of a true human being, entire in what belongs to him and entire in what belongs to us.

By the expression "what belongs to us" we mean the things which the Creator established in us from the beginning and which he took on himself for the sake of restoring them. Of those things which the Deceiver introduced [into human existence] and which a deceived humanity accepted, there was no trace in the Savior. No more does the fact that he shared human weaknesses signify that he had a part in our evil actions. He took on the form of a slave without any spot of sin. What he did was to enhance humanity not diminish deity. That self-emptying of his, by which the invisible revealed himself visible and the Creator and Lord of all things elected to be reckoned among mortals, was a drawing-near in mercy not a failure in power.

Consequently, he who made humanity while remaining in the form of God is the same one who in the form of a slave became human. Each nature retained its characteristics without defect, and just as the "form of God" does not remove the "form of a slave," so the "form of a slave" does not diminish the "form of God."

Here was the devil, boasting—that humankind, deceived by his lie, had lost God's gifts and undergone the hard sentence of death after being stripped of its endowment of immortality; that he himself, in the midst of his troubles, had derived some comfort from the fact that he had a partner in his transgression; and, what is more, that God, by reason of the claim of justice, had altered his judgment of humanity even though he had created it in such honor. In the face of all this, there had to be, in God's secret purpose, a way of dealing with this problem, in order that the immutable God, whose will cannot be deprived of the beneficence proper to it, might by a more hidden gift of grace fulfill his original gracious intention with regard to humanity, and also in order that humanity, which had been led into guilt by the devil's craft, might not perish in contradiction to God's purpose.

(4) So it is that God's Son enters this lower world. He descends from his heavenly throne and is born with a new kind of birth in a novel order of existence, yet without departing from the glory of his Father.

The mode of existence is novel because one who is invisible in his own way of being has become visible in ours, and because the incomprehensible has willed to be understood. While continuing to be beyond time, he begins to exist from a point in time. Veiling his measureless majesty, the Lord of the universe assumes the "form of a slave." The impassible God does not disdain existence as a passible human being, and the immortal does not disdain to submit himself to the laws of death.

He is born with a new kind of birth, because an inviolate virginity, unacquainted with desire, supplied the matter of his flesh. What the Lord took from his mother was nature, not guilt. The fact that his birth was extraordinary does not mean that our Lord Jesus Christ, in his birth of a virgin, has a nature different from ours. The same one who is a genuine human being is also genuinely God, and in this unity there is no deception as long as both lowliness and divine loftiness have their reciprocal spheres. Just as

149

God is not altered by his compassion, so humanity is not destroyed by its elevation in honor.

Each "form" carries on its proper activities in communion with the other. The Word does what belongs to it, and the flesh carries out what belongs to it. The one shimmers with wondrous deeds, the other succumbs to injury and insult. Just as the Word does not withdraw from the glory which it shares equally with the Father, neither does the flesh surrender the nature of humankind, for there is one and the same—as we must say over and over again—who is genuinely Son of God and genuinely Son of man. He is God by reason of the fact that "in the beginning was the Word, and the Word was with God, and the Word was God" [John 1:1]. He is human by reason of the fact that "the Word was made flesh and dwelt among us" [John 1:14]. He is God by reason of the fact that "all things have been made through him, and without him nothing was made" [John 1:3]. He is human by reason of the fact that "he was made out of a woman, made under the law" [Gal. 4:4].

The fact that it was flesh which was born reveals his human nature, while the fact that he was born of a virgin gives evidence of the divine power. The state of infancy proper to a child is exhibited by the meanness of his cradle; the greatness of the Most High is declared by the voices of the angels. The one whom Herod sets out to kill is like an ungrown human being, but the one whom the Magi worship with humble joy is the Lord of all. Lest the fact that his flesh was the veil of deity go unrecognized, the voice of God thundered from heaven as early as the time at which he came to the baptism ministered by his forerunner John: "This is my beloved Son, in whom I am well pleased" [Matt. 3:17]. So the one whom the devil's cunning tempted as a human being is the same one to whom the angel's services were rendered as God. Plainly it is a human thing to hunger and thirst and get tired and sleep. But to satisfy five thousand men with bread and to bestow on a Samaritan woman living water whose consumption enables its drinker to thirst no more, to walk on the surface of the sea without sinking and to moderate "the swellings of the waves" when a storm has come up—that is a divine thing without question. But let us pass over much of the evidence and sum the matter up. It is not an act of one and the same nature to weep over a friend's death in an access of pity and to summon that very friend back to life with the power of a word after opening the grave in which he had been buried for four days; or to hang from the cross and to cause the stars to tremble in their courses after turning day into night; or to be pierced with nails and to open the gates of paradise to the faith of a thief. By the same token, it is not an act of one and the same nature to say, "I and the Father are one" [John 10:30], and to say "The Father is greater than I" [John 14:28]. Even though there is, in our Lord Jesus Christ, one person of God and of a human being, nevertheless the principle in virtue of which both share in indignity is one thing, and the principle in virtue of which both share in glory is another. A humanity inferior to the Father comes to him from us, and a divinity equal to the Father's comes to him from the Father.

(5) Because of this unity of person, which must be understood to subsist in a twofold nature, we read that the Son of man came down from heaven (since the Son of God took on flesh from the Virgin of whom he was born), and conversely we say that the Son of God was crucified and buried (even though he endured these things not in that divine nature in virtue of which, as Only Begotten, he is coeternal and consubstantial with the Father, but in the weakness of his human nature). Consequently we all also confess in the creed that the only-begotten Son was crucified and buried, in accordance with the words of the apostle: "For if they had known, they would never have crucified the Lord of glory" [1 Cor. 2:8]. What is more, when our Lord and Savior himself was informing the faith of his disciples by the questions he asked them, he said, "Who do people say that I, the Son of man, am?" And when they had repeated the various opinions of others to him, he went on, "But who do you say that I am?"—I who am Son of man and whom you perceive in "the form of a slave" and in the reality of my flesh—"who do you say that I am?" [Matt. 16:13–18]. At this point the blessed Peter, divinely inspired and about to help the nations by his confession said, "You are the Christ, the Son of

151

the living God." And it was not undeserved that the Lord called him blessed and that Peter took the firmness both of his power and of his name from the original Rock—this man who, through revelation of the Father, confessed that the same person was both Son of God and Christ; for if one of these affirmations is received without the other, it does not profit for salvation. It was equally perilous for people to believe that the Lord Jesus Christ is simply God and not a human being, or a mere human being and not God.

Consider the time after the Lord's resurrection (which was the resurrection of a real body, for none other was revived than the one who was crucified and done to death). For what other reason was there a waiting period of forty days than that the wholeness of our faith might be cleansed from all obscurity? He spoke with his disciples and lived and ate together with them, and permitted himself to be handled by the eager, searching touch of those who were troubled by doubts. This is the reason he entered into his disciples' company through closed doors and conferred the Holy Spirit by the breath of his mouth and, when he had given the light of understanding, opened the hidden things of the Holy Scriptures. On the other hand, the same person exhibited all the evidences of his recent suffering—the wound in his side and the prints of the nails—and said, "See by my hands and my feet that it is I. Touch and see; for a spirit does not have flesh and bones as you see that I have" [Luke 24:39].

Why was all this? In order that the characteristic properties of the divine and human natures might be acknowledged to persist in him without separation, and in order that we might grasp the difference between Logos and flesh in such a way as to confess that the Son and Logos of God, on the one hand, and the flesh, on the other, are one reality.

Our Eutyches must be judged entirely innocent of this mystery of faith. In God's Only Begotten he does not acknowledge the presence of our nature, whether in the humility of the mortal state or in the glory of the resurrection life. Nor has Eutyches trembled before the judgment of the blessed apostle and evangelist John: "Every spirit which confesses that Jesus Christ came in the flesh is of God, and any spirit which dissolves Jesus is not of God, and this is Antichrist'' [1 John 4:2, 3]. But what is meant by "dissolving" Jesus if not to separate his human nature from him and so, by shameless fiction, to render the mystery by which alone we are saved null and void? Surely if he obscures the nature of Christ's body he must also, by reason of the same blindness, play the fool where Christ's suffering is concerned. If he does not think that the Lord's cross is a sham, and if he does not doubt that the punishment borne by Christ for the world's salvation was real, let him acknowledge the flesh of the one whose death he affirms. And let him not deny that one whom he knows to have been capable of suffering was a human being with our sort of body, for if you reject real flesh, you reject corporeal suffering. If, then, he accepts the Christian faith and is not deaf to the preaching of the Gospel, let him ask himself which nature was pierced by nails and hung on the wood of the cross, and let him understand from what source the "blood and water" flowed, when the soldier's lance pierced the side of the crucified one so that the church might be moistened both by washing and by the cup. What is more, let him hear the blessed apostle Peter proclaiming that "sanctification of the Spirit" comes through "the sprinkling of the blood of Christ" [1 Pet. 1:2]. And let him read—and attentively, too—the words of the same apostle when he says, "Knowing that it is not by corruptible gold and silver that you have been redeemed from the vain way of life practiced by your fathers, but by the precious blood of a pure and spotless lamb, Jesus Christ" [1 Pet. 1:18–19]. Nor let him stand against the testimony of the blessed apostle John, who says, "And may the blood of Jesus the Son of God cleanse you from all sin" [1 John 1:7]. And again, "This is the victory which overcomes the world, even our faith" [1 John 5:5]. Furthermore, "Who is it that overcomes the world except the one who believes that Jesus is the Son of God? This is the one who came by water and by blood, even Jesus Christ—not by water only, but by water and by blood. And it is the Spirit who bears witness, because the Spirit is truth, for there are three which bear witness—the Spirit, the water, and the blood—and the three are one" [1 John 5:6–8].

This means the Spirit of sanctification and the blood of redemption and the water of baptism. These three are one, they remain undivided, and none of them exists in separation from the others. The catholic church lives and grows by the faith that in Christ Jesus there is neither humanity apart from real divinity nor divinity apart from real humanity.

(6) When Eutyches responded to your questions by saying, "I confess that before the union our Lord was of two natures, but after the union I confess one nature," I am astounded that this quite absurd and quite perverse profession of his went uncensured by any rebuke from his judges and that an utterly foolish and blasphemous expression was passed over as if nothing offensive had been heard. It is just as irreverent to say that the Son of God was of two natures before the incarnation as it is execrable to say that after "the Logos was made flesh" the nature which is in him is one in number. In case Eutyches thinks that since you said nothing to repudiate it this statement of his asserted something correct and tolerable, I admonish your earnest sense of duty, dear brother, that if, through the inspiration of God's mercy, this case is brought to a satisfactory conclusion, the imprudence of an inexperienced person may be purged of this intellectual virus too. As the minutes reveal, he did in fact begin to depart from his ideas. Compelled by your judgment, he professed himself an assertor of what he had not said earlier and a believer in that faith from which he had previously departed. Since, however, he declined to agree to the necessity of anathematizing the irreverent teaching, Your Fraternity understood that he remained in his faithlessness and that he was worthy of condemnation. So if he is genuinely and fruitfully sorry, and comes to a tardy recognition of how rightly episcopal authority was moved to take action, or at any rate, to make full satisfaction, condemns with his own voice and his accompanying signature all the ideas which he wrongly conceived, no degree of mercy will be blamable in the case of one who has mended his ways. Our Lord, the true and good shepherd, who "laid down his life for his sheep" [John 10:15] and who "came to save people's souls, not to lose" them [Luke 9:56], wants us to be imitators of his faithful-

ness, so that justice may indeed compel those who are sinning, but mercy may not turn the repentant away. Our faith will finally be defended to good purpose when the false opinion is condemned even by its adherents. I have, however, given directions to my brothers Julius the bishop and Renatus the presbyter, as well as to my son Hilary the deacon, to act in my stead, so that the case may be settled reverently and faithfully. With them I have associated my notary Dulcitius, whose reliability has been established. I am confident that God's help will be available, so that this man who had sinned may be saved when he has condemned his depraved idea.

May God keep you unharmed, dearest brother.

Given on the Ides of June, in the consulship of the honorable Asturius and the honorable Protogenes.

THE COUNCIL OF CHALCEDON'S "DEFINITION OF THE FAITH"

The holy and great and ecumenical synod, gathered in virtue of God's grace and at the command of our pious and Christ-loving emperors, the Augusti Marcian and Valentinian, in Chalcedon, metropolis of the eparchy of Bithynia, in the martyry of the holy and triumphant martyr Euphemia, has laid down the following decrees.

Our Lord and Savior Jesus Christ, as he was establishing his disciples in understanding of the faith, stated, "My peace I leave with you, my peace I give to you" [John 14:27], in order that no one should speak differently from his neighbor about the teachings of true religion, but that, on the contrary, the proclamation of the faith should be exhibited as the same for all.

Since the evil one does not cease using his tares to plant over the seeds of true religion and is always discovering something against the truth, the Lord, for this reason, with his customary providential care for the human race, raised this most pious and faithful emperor to zeal and convoked the leaders of the priesthood from every quarter to himself, so that as the grace of Christ, the Lord of us all,

155

was working, every defilement of falsehood might be removed from Christ's sheep and she might be enriched by the plantings of truth.

And this we have done. By unanimous vote we have driven away the teachings of error, and we have renewed the inerrant faith of the Fathers. We have proclaimed to all the Symbol of the Three Hundred and Eighteen and we have endorsed, as belonging to the same family, the Fathers who accepted that covenant of true religion—we mean the one hundred and eighty who subsequently assembled in the great city of Constantinople and themselves validated the same faith.

We therefore decree (keeping to the ranking and to all the decisions about the faith established by the holy synod which met at Ephesus under the leadership of Celestine of Rome and Cyril of Alexandria, of blessed memory) that primary authority shall belong to the exposition of the correct and blameless faith composed by the three hundred and eighteen holy and blessed fathers who gathered in Nicaea when Constantine, of devout memory, was emperor; and that authority shall belong to the decrees which derive from the one hundred and eighty holy fathers in Constantinople, which they laid down for the destruction of the heresies which had grown up at that time and for the corroboration of our same catholic and apostolic faith.

The Symbol of the 318 at Nicaea

"We believe in one God, Father, Ruler of all, the maker of heaven and earth and of all things seen and unseen.

"And in one Lord Jesus Christ, the only-begotten Son of God, begotten from the Father before all ages, true God from true God, begotten not made, of one essence with the Father; through whom all things were made; who for us human beings and for our salvation came down and was incarnate and became human; and suffered, and rose on the third day and went up into the heavens and is seated at the right hand of the Father, and is coming to judge the living and the dead.

"And in the Holy Spirit.

"But those who say, 'There was a "when" when he was not'

and 'Before he was begotten he did not exist' and 'He came into existence out of nothing,' or who say that the Son of God is 'from another hypostasis or essence,' or 'mutable' or 'alterable'—them the catholic and apostolic church anathematizes.''

The Symbol of the 180 at Constantinople

"We believe in one God, Father, Ruler of all, Maker of heaven and earth and of all things visible and invisible.

"And in one Lord Jesus Christ, the only-begotten Son of God, begotten from the Father before all ages, Light from Light, true God from true God, begotten not made, of one essence with the Father, through whom all things were made; who for us human beings and for our salvation came down from heaven and was incarnate from the Holy Spirit and Mary the Virgin and became human; and was crucified for us under Pontius Pilate, and suffered, and was buried, and rose on the third day in accordance with the Scriptures; and went up into the heavens, and is seated at the right hand of the Father, and is coming again with glory to judge the living and the dead. His Kingdom will have no end.

"And in the Holy Spirit, the Lord, the Lifegiver, who proceeds from the Father, who is worshiped and glorified together with the Father and the Son, who spoke through the prophets: in one holy catholic and apostolic church. We confess one baptism for the remission of sins. We expect the resurrection of the dead and the life of the coming world.''

This wise and saving symbol of the divine grace should have been sufficient for the knowledge and support of true religion, for it gives the complete teaching about the Father and the Son and the Holy Spirit, and to those who receive it faithfully it interprets the Lord's becoming human. Nevertheless, since those who attempt to set aside the proclamation of the truth have given birth to empty talk through their own heresies (some daring to corrupt the mystery of the Lord's dispensation on our behalf and deny the title "Mother of God" to the Virgin, others introducing a confusion and mixture, and stupidly imagining that there is one nature of the flesh and the deity, and suggesting impossibly that in virtue of this confusion the divine nature of the Only Begotten is passible): for this reason, this holy, great, and ecumenical synod now assembled, seeking to deprive them of every device against the truth, and teaching the ever-unchanging character of the proclamation, has decreed in the first place that the Creed of the Three Hundred and Eighteen holy fathers shall stand untouched. Furthermore, because of those who take up arms against the Holy Spirit, it confirms the teaching about the essence of the Spirit which was later handed down by the one hundred and eighty holy fathers gathered in the imperial city. They made this teaching known to everyone, not by adding anything which was left out by their predecessors but by clarifying, through scriptural testimonies, their understanding of the Holy Spirit in opposition to those who were trying to reject his rule.

And because of those who attempt to corrupt the mystery of the dispensation, shamelessly pretending that the one born of the holy Mary was an ordinary human being, it has received, as in agreement [with this faith], the synodical letters of the blessed Cyril, then shepherd of the Alexandrian church, to Nestorius and the Orientals, for the sake of refuting the follies of Nestorius and for the instruction of those who, in religious zeal, seek understanding of the saving Symbol.

With these letters, for the confirmation of the orthodox teachings, it has appropriately included the letter which the most blessed and holy archbishop Leo, who presides in the great and elder Rome, wrote to the holy archbishop Flavian for the removal of the error of Eutyches, for it agrees with the confession of the great Peter and is a common pillar against those who think wrongly.

For [this synod] sets itself against those who attempt to split up the mystery of the dispensation into a duality of sons; and those who dare to assert that the deity of the Only Begotten is passible it expels from the college of priests; and it opposes those who conceive of a confusion or mixture in the case of the two natures of Christ; and it drives out those who foolishly think that the "form of a slave" which was assumed by him from among us is of a heavenly, or some other, essence; and it anathematizes those who make up the teaching that before the union there are two natures of the Lord, but imagine that after the union there is one.

158

Following, therefore, the holy fathers, we confess one and the same Son, who is our Lord Jesus Christ, and we all agree in teaching that this very same Son is complete in his deity and complete—the very same—in his humanity, truly God and truly a human being, this very same one being composed of a rational soul and a body, coessential with the Father as to his deity and coessential with us—the very same one—as to his humanity, being like us in every respect apart from sin. As to his deity, he was born from the Father before the ages, but as to his humanity, the very same one was born in the last days from the Virgin Mary, the Mother of God, for our sake and the sake of our salvation: one and the same Christ, Son, Lord, Only Begotten, acknowledged to be unconfusedly, unalterably, undividedly, inseparably in two natures, since the difference of the natures is not destroyed because of the union, but on the contrary, the character of each nature is preserved and comes together in one person and one hypostasis, not divided or torn into two persons but one and the same Son and only-begotten God, Logos, Lord Jesus Christ—just as in earlier times the prophets and also the Lord Jesus Christ himself taught us about him, and the symbol of our Fathers transmitted to us.

Since, therefore, these matters have been determined by us with all possible precision and care, the holy and ecumenical synod decrees that it is not permissible for anyone to propose, write, compose, think, teach anything else. But those who dare to compose another creed or to bring forward or teach or transmit another symbol to people who want to turn to the knowledge of truth from Hellenism or Judaism or from any heresy whatever—such persons, if they are bishops or clergy, are deposed, the bishops from their episcopate and the clergy from their office; but if they are monks or laity they are anathematized.

Bibliography

Bright, W., ed. *The Orations of Saint Athanasius against the Arians.* Oxford: At the Clarendon Press, 1884.

Cullmann, O. *The Christology of the New Testament.* Translated by S. C. Guthrie and C. Hall. Philadelphia: Westminster Press, 1959.

Daniélou, J. *Origen.* Translated by W. Mitchell. New York: Sheed & Ward, 1955.

Fuller, R. H. *The Foundations of New Testament Christology.* New York: Scribner, 1965.

Greer, R. A. *The Captain of Our Salvation.* Tübingen: J. C. B. Mohr, 1973.

Grillmeier, A. *Christ in Christian Tradition.* Translated by J. Bowden. 2d ed. Atlanta: John Knox Press and London: Mowbray, 1975.

Hahn, F. *The Titles of Jesus in Christology.* Translated by H. Knight and G. Ogg. New York: World Publishing Co., 1969.

Kelly, J. N. D. *Early Christian Doctrines,* 5th rev. ed. London: A. & C. Black, 1977 and New York: Harper & Row, 1978.

Koetschau, P., ed. *Origenes Werke,* vol. 5: *De Principiis (Die Griechischen christlichen Schriftsteller der ersten drei Jahrhunderte,* vol. 22), Leipzig: J. C. Hinrichs, 1913.

Kroymann, E., ed. *Q. S. Fl. Tertulliani de carne Christi,* in *Corpus Christianorum,* Series Latina, vol. 2: *Tertulliani Opera.* Turnholt, 1954.

_____ and E. Evans, eds. *Q. S. Fl. Tertulliani adversus Praxean,* in *Corpus Christianorum,* Series Latina, vol. 2: *Tertulliani Opera.* Turnholt, 1954.

Lietzmann, H. *Apollinaris von Laodicea und seine Schule.* Tübingen: J. C. B. Mohr, 1904.

Loofs, F., ed. *Nestoriana: Die Fragmente des Nestorius.* Halle: Max Niemeyer, 1905.

161

Moule, C. F. D. *The Origin of Christology.* Cambridge: At the University Press, 1977.

Norris, R. A., Jr. *Manhood and Christ: A Study in the Christology of Theodore of Mopsuestia.* Oxford: Clarendon Press, 1963.

Pannenberg, W. *Jesus God and Man.* Philadelphia: Westminster Press, 1968.

Pelikan, J. *The Light of the World.* New York: Harper, 1962.

──────. *The Christian Tradition,* vol. 1: *The Emergence of the Catholic Tradition.* Chicago: University of Chicago Press, 1971.

Perler, O., ed. *Sur la Pâque et fragments* [par] *Méliton de Sardes.* Paris: Éditions du Cerf, 1966.

Pollard, T. E. *Johannine Christology and the Early Church.* Cambridge: At the University Press, 1970.

Prestige, G. L. *Fathers and Heretics.* London: S.P.C.K., 1963.

Sagnard, F., ed. *Irenaeus: Contre les hérésies.* Paris: Éditions du Cerf, 1952–69.

Schwartz, E., ed. *Acta Conciliorum Oecumenicorum.* Berlin and Leipzig: De Gruyter, 1914ff.

Sellers, R. V. *Two Ancient Christologies.* London: S.P.C.K., 1954.

──────. *The Council of Chalcedon.* London: S.P.C.K., 1953.

Swete, H.B., ed. *Theodori Episcopi Mopsuesteni in Epistolas B. Pauli Commentarii.* 2 vols. Cambridge: At the University Press, 1880. (Vol. 2 contains an edition of Theodore's dogmatic fragments.)

Wingren, G. *Man and the Incarnation: A Study in the Biblical Theology of Irenaeus.* Philadelphia: Muhlenberg (now Fortress) Press and Edinburgh: Oliver and Boyd, 1959.